PRECOCIOUS BROWN EYES

MARIAN HUNTER
&
GLORIA KING

ISBN: 978-1-950649-59-4
Cover: Life Chronicles Publishing

Photo Credit: Rosetta Knight

Life Chronicles Publishing Copyright © 2021

lifechroniclespublishing.com

All rights reserved. No part of this book may be reproduced in any form or by any electronic or mechanical means, including information storage and retrieval systems, with or without permission from the publisher or author, except in the case of a review, whereas quotes of a brief passage embodied in critical articles or in a review.

This book is especially dedicated to my family, who helped me gather and put the events in order as my mother intended.

Thank you to my daughter, V. Lynne Reese, for your untiring work with typing, formatting, proofreading, and late-night phone calls. Without you, this book would still be in the making.

Thank you to my husband, R H King, who put up with the scattered papers around the living room and my long hours at the computer.

A special thank you to Rosetta Knight for her photo cover contribution.

Marian Hunter & Gloria King

Table of Contents

Introduction 1
Chapter 1 3
Chapter 2 9
Chapter 3 15
Chapter 4 25
Chapter 5 34
Chapter 6 41
Chapter 7 49
Chapter 8 61
Chapter 9 69
Chapter 10 79
Chapter 11 85
Chapter 12 107
Chapter 13 117
Chapter 14 125
Chapter 15 135
Chapter 16 147
About the Authors 153

Marian Hunter & Gloria King

Introduction

Precocious Brown Eyes is a delightful, yet thoughtful look at what life was like growing up in the Pacific Northwest in the early 20s through the 40s for a black family. Some situations demanded quick wit and innovative measures to maintain their existence.

This book is a heart-wrenching story of a young girl discovering the circumstances of her birth and the search to find her biological father. In short, it is the intriguing way life was viewed through the eyes of a special little girl who refused to grow up.

Marian Hunter & Gloria King

Chapter 1

Cris was 51 years old, tall and slim, even considered skinny by some standards. A sprinkling of grey was beginning to show in her thick mahogany hair, which she usually wore neatly plaited in a large French braid. Her figure belied her years. In fact, it was the envy of most of her contemporaries and by some who were years her junior. Although her face was small, oval, and unlined as yet, she was not in the least beautiful. Her too broad and slightly flattened nose (due to a childhood mishap) destroyed that illusion. She wasn't pretty. Although that concept was quickly removed when one looked at her generous mouth, she was attractive in a fascinating way. This fascination was due to her lithe animal grace and her eyes.

Her eyes were the mirror of her innermost self; people said they were *Precocious Brown Eyes*. These eyes reflected her every mood from the deepest sorrow to moments of ecstasy. They were large, wide-set, and almond-shaped, fringed by long sooty lashes and crowned by slightly arched brows. They were soft and brown, full of love, understanding, and would seemingly pierce through you. Sometimes they were hard and cold, filled with determination or hatred, yet young and gay, dancing with life and mischief or merriment. They were old and lifeless, disarmingly naive or warily shrewd. Her eyes were indeed the mirror of her innermost being and precisely reflected the emotion most auspicious for her at any given moment. Her control of them was perfect.

Cris possessed a quick analytical, computer-like mind. Many bits of pertinent information were compactly filed away, ready for instant recall, when needed or rather when and if advantageous to her. She was basically a truthful person, having learned years ago that the truth could raise grave doubts of its veracity in the listener's mind if told with the right inflections. Therefore, idle gossip or lies, per se, bored her.

She learned to be witty and nonsensical even when she would have much preferred the solitude of a good book or the mental stimuli of a lively discussion of current events. Her sense of humor helped her through many rough spots in her life. Sometimes she was able to turn a misfortune into an amusing incident. She had few confidants but was the confidant of many. She was an interesting person because of her curiosity about others. That keen curiosity was only known to her.

Being a meticulous housekeeper, the monotony of routine household chores escaped her. If not for this idiosyncrasy, she was your typical average, middle-aged, middle-class American female and would have been so classified, except CRIS WAS BLACK!! There were no typical classifications for her!

Cris automatically touched the brakes of the Oldsmobile lightly before turning onto the avenue leading home. (It was just another street, but the word avenue pleased her better. It made it sound richer - more elite.) She drove slowly, letting her gaze wander over the lake and beyond it to the verdant hills. It was a beautiful spring afternoon, and the car was pleasantly warm. Nevertheless, she felt a chill creep over her. She knew it was because she allowed her mind's eye to picture the cemetery that was in those hills. The hills where Gram now slept. She remembered the disagreeably cold, raw afternoon Gram had been laid to rest there and thinking, "*not in this damp half-frozen ground. Gram liked to be warm.*" Then the next thought, "Oh, God, why now? Now when I haven't done any of the things for her, I wanted."

On the ride back to town, she remembered feeling cheated and guilty. Cheated because there was no time now and guilty because she knew she hadn't done what she could when she had the time to do it. Impetuously, she pulled over to the curb and stopped where the view was unobstructed of the lake, bridge, as well as the verdant hills beyond them. The calm waters of the lake reflected the blueness of the sky. Here sailboats dotted its surface, their gleaming white sails straining to catch the faint breeze. She noticed traffic on the bridge was sparse and too early for the commuters. After smoking a cigarette, she pulled out into traffic again.

Now she was abreast of the Monroe house, and she wished they were still living there. It would be so nice to drop in for a cup of coffee and a light talk with Sue. It would take her mind off things she was not yet ready to remember. The new owners were puttering in the yard. They called out a warm greeting to her and had the air of expecting her to stop. Precocious Brown Eyes waved to them but kept on her way slowly. They were a nice enough couple, alright, but somehow she had the feeling they were not her kind. Not her kind. The phrase stuck in her mind pushing other thoughts into the background for the time being. That was something worth thinking about. Just who was her kind anyway?

She signaled to turn into the driveway of her home, then abruptly changed her mind and stopped in front of the house. She sat there, looking at her house as if she were seeing it for the first time. It was a neat, compact brick house set back from the street and approached by a winding stairway and a curving walk. She looked at the rockery and mentally noted to trim the heather and get those dandelions out. (Hope I have some weedkiller left.) Not a bad house, she mused, although the trim needs painting and a new roof is an essential need to be taken care of soon, but yet, alright, which means to her substantial and relatively prosperous looking. It was not large or pretentious, but it was ample for her needs. The daffodils bordering the driveway were gone, but the tulips were putting on a good show. (H'm, must put something else in there for later color.) She noticed the azaleas were bursting into rich red, vibrant blooms, and the roses were coming along nicely.

Baron's welcoming bark broke the trance. She had things to do. Enough of this wool-gathering for one afternoon. Quickly gathering up her packages, she hurried into the house. Baron greeted her with all the exuberance only a Shepherd pup possesses. Laughingly she scolded him. "Down, Baron, sit. You'll get your goodie as soon as I get down to it." He sat, sweeping the floor with his tail and watching her expectantly until she handed him a large meaty bone. Grasping it in his mouth, he went to the back door to be let out. Cris gave him a playful slap as he passed her. Precocious Brown Eyes busied herself putting groceries away and making coffee. Then she stood at the window watching the dog worry his bone while the coffee perked. The Early Edition of the news was on when she finally strolled into the living room and switched on the TV. Placing her cup of steaming coffee on the lamp table and her feet on the ottoman, she was ready to relax with the evening news.

Although she appeared comfortable and relaxed, she was uncomfortable, uneasy, and unable to relax. That nagging phrase 'her kind' was yet bothering her. There she sat, listening and not hearing, looking but not seeing. When the news was over, she returned to the kitchen to prepare dinner for herself and Baron.

She was not hungry; however, knowing Baron, he would be voraciously hungry. That, it seemed, was his perpetual state of being. He was a growing puppy and needed to eat. To her past query of how big he would become and how much he would eventually weigh on reaching his full growth, the Vet teasingly answered, "ordinarily, not much bigger, and he should weigh between 90 and 100 pounds. Baron will be between 120 and 130. Don't overfeed him. He's way overweight now." Then he had gone on earnestly, "Believe me, Mrs. Dermond, you're unfair to him by overfeeding him." She knew what he said was true...but...Baron liked to eat. Cris sat at the table, toyed with her meat, piled the potatoes in mounds, and carefully separated peas and carrots. She did eat the avocado slices out of her salad. Baron wolfed his dinner down and then came to sit at her side at the table, waiting patiently for the food on her plate he was sure he would get. And he did.

Her dishes were carefully rinsed and placed in the dishwasher, and then the rest of the kitchen was tidied before she left. Cleaning the kitchen was a mechanical procedure with Cris. "One never knows what's going to happen in the night or any other time for that matter, and you never know when someone's going to have to come in to do something for you." That was ingrained in her early in childhood by Gram. She paused in the dining room to rearrange the flowers and took an approving glance around the room. It passed her inspection, almost. The mirror above the buffet was clean and unstreaked. The silver tea set gleaming and untarnished. The china and crystal behind the spotless glass of the china cabinet shining and bright. The wood of the furniture waxed and well-polished. The flaw... the chandelier. She would have preferred a more ornate one—the drapes adjusted to her satisfaction.

She crossed the small entry hall and through the arch into the living room. Unconsciously she straightened a magazine on the coffee table in passing. She continued to the rows of books flanking the fireplace, then idly thumbed through several books before selecting one for her evening reading. To the casual observer, Cris appeared unaware of the graciousness of the room. You would immediately know that this room was very carefully planned and arranged to the more observant. The large mirror over the fireplace reproduced faithfully the plushness of the sage green crushed velvet sofa, the green and white cut velvet Mr. And Mrs. Chairs, and the artfully smacked pillows nestled on them. Her creative lamps and the burnished beauty of the leather-topped tables. The uniqueness of the kidney-shaped bench covered the lustrous green brocade, which was placed invitingly in front of the fireplace. Oh, yes, Cris was quite aware of how this room looked and its impression on most people seeing it for the first time. Before settling down to read, she flipped the dial on the TV to phono, not bothering to check the records on the spindle. The muted sound of the music filled the room. She turned on the reading lamp, preparatory to an enjoyable evening. She leaned her head on the back of the chair and closed her eyes. She thought, "I'll just listen to the music briefly before I put the car up and then read," but the music unstopped a flood of memories. The book lay forgotten and unopened in her lap while Baron lay at her feet.

Chapter 2

In a city or even a town it would have been a corner lot, but, here, it was the beginning of nowhere.

The small brown house sat almost on the ground in a tiny, cleared space. In the summer, the land around it was parched, dry, dusty, and a field of mud in the winter. The house was old and weather-beaten, but around the one step leading to the house's front porch, a few plants and flowers struggled for survival. A stone's throw from the back door of the house was the outhouse. The pathway leading to it was carefully outlined with rocks, as was the pathway leading away from the front porch and around the house. In the front of the house was a road that dwindled off to nothing. It was about a good stone's throw away. To the right of the house, beyond a thick growth of huckleberry bushes and hazelnut trees, was another road in similar condition. The difference being, this road had deeper ruts and was, therefore, dustier or muddier, depending on the time of year. Also, this one led somewhere. Motor cars used it as an alternate route to the main cluster of houses which began about six blocks east of the little brown house. Six blocks east of the little brown house, the streets were paved or asphalt-covered and cement sidewalks. The roads over there were wide enough for two cars to pass without one taking to the bushes. There were two general stores (where you could buy almost anything except furniture) and a meat market. You were at the hourly trolley line if you traveled eight blocks west of the little brown house. You could either take the seven-mile ride into town or the two-and-a-half-mile ride to the end of the line into the park.

The only other house on the block was a neat 'story.' It was a half-white frame house trimmed with gray-green paint enclosed behind an equally cute white-washed picket fence. There was no outhouse in the rear of this house. Instead, it had a garage which was used as a storage or tool shed. There were flowers and a lawn in the yard, plus a swing on the long front porch.

There was no fence around the little brown house. It fell long ago and been cut and stacked thriftily beside the back door to supplement the supply of stove wood. The house had a box-like structure, divided into four compartments or rooms. The two larger divisions were the living room and the kitchen; the two smaller were the bedrooms. The floors were bare and scrubbed 'clean enough to eat off' was the expression oft-heard about this little house. The furnishings were exiguous, old, and mismatched but adequate for the need if not for the users' comfort. A sofa covered with a scrupulously clean faded coverlet, a high-backed wooden rocker, its unyielding seat made a bit more comfortable by a pillow, a straight wooden chair of unknown vintage, and a small table which was graced by a kerosene lamp. (The lamp was always well filled, the wick carefully trimmed, and the chimney gleaming.) This was the living room.

The more oversized bedrooms contained two small beds with white iron bedsteads—the aisle way between the beds covered with a colorful rag rug. A flowered cretonne curtain hung at the room's only window, and another piece of the same material hung across one corner of the room, forming a makeshift closet. A large trunk occupied the other corner. Between the beds was a small table (cretonne-covered orange crate) holding the room's means of illumination; a kerosene lamp.

The smaller bedroom contained only one large bed, a rag rug beside it, a table (cretonne-covered orange crate), and a foot locker. The window was cretonne-covered with a piece that hung to form a closet across one corner of the room. This room had no lamp because children slept there, and a lamp was considered too dangerous.

And, lastly, the kitchen. The massive black range with the bright chrome trim dominated the room. The stove served for cooking purposes and the house's water heater and the heating unit. It was a large overhead warming oven which almost always held some delicious tidbit. An oil-cloth-covered table with three mismatched chairs and an apple box, topped by a gray pillow, made up the seating and dining space. Wall shelves and a tall old fashioned kitchen cabinet held the spartan supply of dishes and cooking utensils and part of the foodstuff. Auxiliary space was adroitly achieved by utilizing cretonne camouflaged orange crates. And a cold-only white enameled oblong sink with piped-in water completed the kitchen furnishings.

The kitchen was more than just a place to cook and eat. It was way ahead of its time. It was a true family room, gathering in the evenings to study, talk, sew, or finish up any work or activity leftover from the day. It was here the family bathed in the round galvanized washtub. It also served as the laundry room, and they met for 'togetherness.' It was the true family room.

The kitchen, that wonderful multi-purpose, multi-smelling place, had the unforgettable aroma of freshly baked bread, the fruity fragrance of steaming jelly or jam cooking, and, sometimes, even the soapy smell of boiling clothes. (The boiling of white clothes was a prerequisite for maintaining the whiteness demanded of clothes in this household. Gram and Sooky often commented,

"There's nothing I hate to see worse than dingy, grey-looking clothes that are supposed to be white."

Although not rich in worldly goods and furnishings, the house was far from poor. It was so full of love, understanding, and the unmistakable warmth of genuine caring that one was apt to overlook the scarcity of the more mundane material things. For instance, the walls held no costly oil paintings, but they were adorned with priceless and invaluable childish crayon drawings. It was a clean house made cozy by love, a place that made a house a home. This was the little brown house that Cris clearly remembered. The other places she lived were only faint, elusive, half-remembered recollections with dream-like clarity.

Gram said she couldn't remember the long train ride from Wyoming to Seattle, but Cris insisted she remember. If she didn't or couldn't remember, how would she know that the porter on the train was summoned in the middle of the night by the chubby finger of Jeanie pressing the buzzer? Gram had been sleeping peacefully when she was awakened by the porter's soft knock and polite query, "May I help you, madam?" Gram assured him she had no need of his service at the time and did not call him. He left, only to return soon with the same question. Gram had been positive something was wrong with his buzzer. She repeated she did not call him. Indeed, something was wrong. Jeanie found the buzzer! Jeanie woke up and, with the natural curiosity bestowed, it seems, on all children, had been exploring her surroundings and consequently found the bell. There she lay, her big mischievous eyes dancing and a dimpled hand suspiciously near the buzzer.

Just Gram, Jeanie, and Cris made the trip. Where was her mother? Oh, yes, she was waiting for them in Seattle with that tall, mustached, taciturn Man. Who was he? Not her or Jeanie's father, but who? Of course, he was her mother's new husband. Their new father. Maybe she did not remember the train trip or the reunion with her mother and the meeting of her new father, but she did remember, vaguely, a house in south Seattle where they had gone. There they met a girl and a boy (much older than she or Jeanie) who was to be her new brother and sister. She remembered they had some pigs and chickens at that house also.

Her memory of the girl faded a bit, but she would never forget the boy. He was mean and ran away from home a lot. And how she wished he would stay away. Once, he put her in with the pigs, for a 'joke' he said. Some joke! She was knocked off her feet by the mother pig and laid there screaming, too terrified to move. Her mother came flying to the rescue, but the Man only laughed and said, "it was only a boyish prank." He must have been mean like his son.

Cris didn't know what pranks the Man played, but she did know her pretty, young mother cried a lot, and most of the time, when he was home, Gram was real quiet.

They did have some good times, though. They would pack a lunch and go to the park or just for a picnic in the woods near their home in nice weather. The girls would run and play, shouting with joy. The boy, Tim, would be busy either bedeviling the girls or trying to elude the watchful eyes of the adults so he could slip away. The Man seldom accompanied them on these outings and when he did, he usually just ate and stretched out in the shade to doze with his head cradled in her mother's lap. Occasionally he would join them in play. It was great fun to watch her tiny mother, so much a young girl, herself, run and play. When he, the Man, did decide to take an active part, he never missed the ball as they did, and if they were racing, he always gave them a good head start but invariably overtook them quickly and effortlessly. Sometimes when he would catch up with her mother, he would pick her up and lightly kiss her before putting her down. These were the good times, but they were few and far and in between.

Most of the time, when he was home, she and Jeanie would be sent to their room and cautioned to play quietly. Gram didn't sing or hum at those times, and her mother's soft brown eyes would be unnaturally bright with unshed tears. Nevertheless, he was a good provider. One morning, after he had gone to work and the older two children were off to school, the two women hastily packed a few belongings, and a moving van came to carry their things away. It hadn't taken long to load because they rushed the packing, and they only took a few essential things like trunks and some of the children's favorite toys. Jeanie and Cris were strangely quiet and subdued during the short inter-city ride. They seemed to sense the urgency and fear the two women tried so vainly to hide. She remembered they stayed briefly in a downtown hotel and then moved here, to the little brown house where there was no gruff Man around. In fact, there was no man, of any temperament around.

Chapter 3

Cris did miss the tangible comforts the Man provided them, but they were all happier without him. As the days lengthened into weeks and then into months, the women gradually lost their harried expressions and laughed and played with them again. She and Jeanie could laugh, shout, shriek, or giggle, as little girls are supposed to do, without being unduly shushed. They enjoyed the freedom and were happy again.

Cris couldn't recall when it happened or just what happened, but by the time they moved to the little brown house, Gram had become 'Mom,' and Mother was 'Sister.' Instinctively, she knew it had something to do with their hasty flight, but she neither knew nor particularly cared to know what it was about.

Even though the house was at the beginning of nowhere, it was the beginning of everything for Cris; it was a new way of life. Her philosophy at that time was: Having a Man in the household meant more material comforts but less happiness.

Mom and Sister (Mom always called her Sooky) had been up before daybreak so they could finish ironing Mrs. Peter's clothes before it got too hot and also because Sooky could drop them off on her way to work if they could finish them in time. Sooky would pick up the dirty laundry on her way home, thus saving herself an extra trip.

The women planned the day's activities as they worked. Mom said, "It's gonna be a scorcher today. They ain't hardly no clouds at all." Sooky just nodded in agreement. She was concentrating on ironing a tricky ruffle at the time. Mom did the basic flat things while Sooky, who was more dexterous, did the fancy pieces. Each time a heated flatiron was lifted from the hot stove, a quick sizzling sound was heard. The women carefully tested each iron with a spit moistened finger to assure it was not too hot and would not scorch the clothes. They both gave a sigh of relief when the last dampened roll was ironed and folded. They stepped out of the opened back door for a breath of fresh air and to cool off. They sat for a short time on the wooden bench beside the opened doorway before Mom said, "Sooky, put the boards away and fix breakfast. You bettah git ready fo' work or you'll be late."

They stood and peered at the cloudless sky momentarily before returning to the stifling kitchen. Mom removed the two ironing boards from the end of the table and the backs of the two chairs they'd been resting on and carefully placed them, face to face, in the corner. Sooky dipped hot water from the back of the stove and carried it into the bedroom for her morning ablution. While Sooky sponged and redressed for work, Mom was busy fixing the breakfast and setting the table. When all was ready, she went to the children's door to awaken them. "Jeanie - Baby, get up now, time to git ready and eat"; "Baby, did you wet that' bed?" Without waiting for an answer, she went on, "Jeanie, I tol' you to wake her up and make her use that pot. "Jeanie, now wide awake, gingerly felt the bed. It was dry, good. Now she wouldn't be scolded for not waking Baby.

Cris had an intense dislike for being called Baby and an even greater hatred for being awakened at night and would refuse to get up more often than not. Consequently, there was frequently a wet bed in the mornings. It wasn't so bad in the summer when the bedding could be washed and hung outside to dry, but the sheets and quilted pad needed to be dried on the lines that were stretched across the kitchen in the winter. Mom didn't like that. Those things took much-needed space to dry her ladies' clothes.

Jeanie stretched lazily and arose. She unfastened the one button at the neck of her little gown and let it slide down her short, plump body to the floor. She knew it went in the dirty clothes this morning and therefore she did not have to be careful with it. Her school clothes had been hung on the foot of the big bed. The stiffly starched dress was still on the hanger. She put on the homemade shift, checking first to see if the drop-seat was all buttoned and next, the little garter belt. (Mom made most of the children's clothes for summer from bleached flour sacks and for winter from flannel outings.) Both materials being cheap and easily obtainable. The sacks sometimes posed a problem because neither bleaching nor boiling would completely obliterate all the trade names imprinted on them. Anyway, Mom reasoned, they were only underclothes and weren't supposed to be seen. Most of their nicer undies, Sunday clothes, boasted wide crocheted edges (just in case they accidentally did show.) All their clothes, play, or dress were neatly ironed and starched, if appropriate.

Neatness and tidiness were placed only second to Godliness in this household (and cleanliness was an absolute must.) She sat on the rag rug to pull on her long, ribbed brown cotton stockings and highly polished shoes; Jeanie smiled, showing her deep dimples, as she reached for her slip. It was her favorite. It was full-skirted and flawlessly starched and ironed. It made her little dresses stand out bell-shaped around her chubby sturdy body. This was all she would put on until after she had eaten and her hair oiled, combed, and precisely braided. Mom and Sooky said she got her dress all wrinkled sitting around in it. They gathered around the kitchen table for breakfast, where four heads bowed humbly, and four pairs of hands were folded primly and thankfully while grace was said. Now that breakfast was over, Sooky and Jeanie donned immaculately clean starched spring dresses and picked up their respective bundles to leave.

Sooky, Mrs. Peter's laundry, Jeanie, and her lard can lunch pail, would walk up the dusty road, as far as the trolley line, and then on to school. Some mornings when there was time, Cris would walk with them. Today, however, there was no time for this because Sooky would have to walk past the trolley line to deliver the laundry and then hurry back to not miss the trolley into town for her day of work.

So today, Mom and Cris stood in the doorway and waved until the huckleberry bushes swallowed up the two departing figures. Sooky had several places she did day work in the wealthier homes in the city. Mom stayed at home to keep house and care for the children, only going out to do day work at the few houses near their home, places she could take Cris whenever she worked. They worked hard, very hard to provide the necessities needed to exist, but they were fiercely proud that they didn't have to ask for or accept welfare aid. They felt they could hold their heads high because they were doing as well as some (most) families where there was both a mother and a father. Their children never went to bed hungry unless they just refused to eat. The meals may not have been epicurean delicacies, but they were skillfully cooked and as well balanced as the larder would allow. At any rate, they were delicious. Mom was an artful cook.

Many were the times' Mom, and Sooky toiled over a large bundle of washing or a huge basket of ironing, working by the flickering light of the kerosene lamp, until the wee hours of the morning. Oft-times, drunk with sheer exhaustion, they would totter to bed for a few pitiable hours of rest and sleep before arising to face another day of the same old drudgery. They firmly believed things would get better. That rosy-hued belief must have sustained them.

This was the family. Four females and each was wrapped in her own thoughts. Mom was thinking, 'it's gonna be hot, real hot. Good day to dry clothes. Sure glad I can put the tubs in the shade. Might as well do ours while I'm at it. Kill two birds with one stone.' Sooky's mind was mentally counting their finances. She was hoping Mr. Peter left the laundry money today. Most of the time, they claimed he forgot it. However, she needed it today because she wanted to buy some shoes for the girls, and fresh meat would certainly be nice for dinner. Jeanie wished school was out so she wouldn't have to wear the long brown cotton stockings she was forced to wear. She reasoned her legs wouldn't get 'ashy' as Mom, Sooky, and Cris said they would. She thought if she greased them well, they wouldn't.

Cris thought her day was ruined. Washday meant she would be expected to gather chips and things to keep the fire going under the boiler. She couldn't pick berries or watch for the car. Her day was completely ruined! Mom placed her tubs outside in what shade the small house afforded. The big copper boiler was perched precariously on large stones over a hallowed place in the ground a few feet from the tubs. A fire was started under the boiler to heat the water needed for the clothes to be boiled.

The clothesline from the house to the outhouse needed to be carefully washed and wiped dry before any clothes could be hung on them. Mom said if they weren't cleaned off, the lines would leave dirty marks on the clothes. Mom and Sooky were well known for producing the whitest, most spotless clothes in the neighborhood. When the preliminary preparations were completed to Mom's satisfaction, she returned to the kitchen to tidy up from breakfast. Cris had long since disappeared into the berry bushes nearby. Maybe today, she would be lucky enough to find some ripe ones. If she did, then Mom could make her a pie. Cris did not have long to explore before she heard Mom call. "Come on now, 'Baby,' get yo' wagon, (a cut-down apple box mounted on small wheels) and pick up some chips an' things to keep the fire going. If we hurry, you'll have plenty time fo' berry picking, if they be any ripe". Reluctantly she scuffed her way back to the house and got her wagon.

Cris worked dutifully and rapidly to build up a sizeable pile of chips, twigs, and small dry branches beside the boiler for a short time. Her interest waned quickly. It was more fun to turn over a chip or stone or watch the beetles, and other small insects scurry for cover. She particularly liked to turn the beetles on their backs and watch their legs flailing in the air, trying to reposition themselves. Sometimes she would mimic their antics and end up weak with laughter and covered with dust. That sport and the trash gathering lasted until she saw Mom straighten from the washtubs and dry her arms on her apron before she laid it in the sun to dry. Now was the time. She scrambled into the bushes and crouched, out of sight, by the side of the road. She knew it was time for the car that she was watching and waiting for; it was a large-shiny open touring Buick. A portly, bespectacled, dark brown-skinned man would be carefully guiding it down the dusty, rutted road. He would desperately and ineffectually try to miss the biggest and deepest ruts to keep the dust to a minimum. The sight always thrilled Cris, and she vowed someday she would have a car like that. When she got her car, she told herself she would sit up straight and tall and be proud to drive, but never, never, would she drive on such a dusty road.

He was coming now, slowly driving as he neared her hiding place. Little Cris thought it was because the road was so bad, but that wasn't the reason at all. He was driving that slowly because he was hoping to get another glimpse of Sooky. He saw her once on a rather windy day when a capricious breeze lifted her skirt, revealing her shapely legs, and pinned it tightly against her small, rounded buttocks. She had been hanging clothes, unaware she was being observed. He liked what he saw and after that spent much time devising ways to meet her.

At various other times, he'd seen the older woman and the two little girls, but he had not been rewarded with another look at Sooky. He was curious about them and had never seen a man around. The place looked to him like the two women, and the children were living there alone. He drove to where the two roads crossed and had a clear view of the house and yard, but he missed out again today. The yard was empty, although it showed signs of recent activity. The lines were filled with impossibly clean clothes. The boiler was steaming over the outdoor fire, and the aroma of strong lye soap was in the air. He drove on to the main street of the settlement and returned to town. Another long ride for nothing. Well, better luck next time.

Sooky stepped lightly from the trolley and daintily picked her way to the sidewalk, where she paused briefly to readjust her packages and for a quick search of her pockets to find something to cover her head. It started to rain shortly before the trolley reached her stop. She neglected to carry an umbrella as it hadn't looked at all like rain when she had gone into town to work. Finding nothing in her quick search, she started walking rapidly down the very muddy road. She skipped nimbly over the large mudholes to the middle of the road, which was less muddy. She earnestly hoped no cars would come by and force her to the side of the road and into the wet bushes to splatter her to boot. Oh, oh, she heard the dreaded sound and the rumble of a motor. She jumped with deer-like grace to the side of the road to wait for the car to pass. It didn't.

The driver brought the big car to a shuddering halt and leaned across the seat to ask politely, "May I give you a ride, Miss? I'm going right your way." She looked up startled, a raindrop sliding off her pert little nose, to see who could possibly be offering her a ride. She didn't know anyone here with a car, and the deep male voice alarmed her. It was not who she feared it might be. It was a portly brown-skinned man. She started to refuse then thought better of her decision. Riding was certainly better than walking in this downpour. "Why yes, thank you." Before the words were spoken, his face beaming with pleasure, he had the door open and was reaching a big strong hand out to help her in the car. Cris was standing at the window alternately watching the raindrops trickle down the windowpane for Sooky. Her eyes opened wide with amazement when the large touring car slithered to a stop in front of the house. Sooky was gallantly lifted out and over a deep puddle in the yard. Cris was speechless, momentarily, but her agile little mind was racing a mile a minute. If Sooky knew that man and could ride in the car, why couldn't she? She wondered if Mom knew Sooky was riding in that car with a man.

"Mom, come here, quick!! Sooky come home in a car!!" Mom was bent over taking biscuits from the oven, but she jack-knifed erect and hastily set the pan in the warming oven to hurry to the window, smoothing her apron-covered dress and hair as she moved. Jeanie was setting the table, but she dropped the silverware in a jumble and almost ran over Mom in her haste to reach the window so she could see too.

"Put that curtain down. Do you want him to think we're from the country and never seen a car before? An' how many times I tol' you to say, 'came home' not 'come home.'" Mom did and could at times lapse into colloquialism, but she was ever on the alert to see that the girls did not. When Sooky reached the sanctuary of the door and stepped inside, she was greeted by three pairs of questioning eyes and a babble of voices. She and Mom exchanged a knowing glance over the children's heads, and Mom returned to the dinner preparations. Before Jeanie and Cris could loose their barrage of questions, Mom put them to work finishing the dinner table setting. Each time they started to ask, they were told not to talk with their mouths full. After dinner, they fared no better and went to bed full of whetted curiosity and unanswered questions, plus an elaborate plan. They planned to stay awake and listen to the talk in the kitchen, so they giggled, plotted, and whispered as they undressed.

Alas, the day's activities had been too thorough. The low drone of the women's voices did nothing but lull them soundly to sleep. Their curiosity could have been so easily satisfied if only they could have stayed awake.

From then on, Mr. Benson became a frequent visitor. Sometimes he would have dinner with them, and at other times he would merely call for Sooky, and they would go out someplace. Occasionally the whole family would be invited to go for a ride to the park or around the waterfront. Now Sooky almost always left and returned from work with Mr. Benson.ee

Marian Hunter & Gloria King

Chapter 4

They moved from the cracker-box brown house into a two-story house in the group of houses that made up the small settlement. The girls were too young to know or understand the scrimping, saving, the corner-cutting, and many deprivations Mom and Sooky had made to be able to make the move. Even then, with all the saving, they would never have been able to afford this large house if, well, that's a story of its own.

They went for a drive with Mr. Benson and saw the vacant house. The owners, an Italian family, seemed anxious to rent it and quoted a moderately low rental price. The women thought they might be able to swing it and often discussed means and ways of doing so.

One night, Mom was sewing, and Sooky's head was bent over the table, close to the kerosene lamp, while she adeptly added and subtracted some figures. The children were blissfully sleeping. "Mom, with my new jobs and the extra washing we're doing, don't you think we can get that house?" said Sooky. Mom finished securing the button on the dress she was mending and deftly snipped the thread with her even white teeth before replying. "We could get it alright, but could we keep it if yo' work falls off or if we lost some of our bundles of laundry, 'specially if we get that washing machine, too?"

"That's just it, Mom. If we get the machine, we will be able to do more laundry and the ironing in much less time. That house is wired for electricity." replied Sooky.

Mom said, "Yeh, that's right, and I'll be able to work more' way from home now since 'Baby' will be going to school." Sooky opened her mouth to say more, thought better of it; she went to the stove and poured herself and Mom some coffee. She returned to sit at the table and stare intently into her cup as if all the answers to her problems would be found inside. Mom furtively watched her and continued her sewing. 'She's got something big on her mind, outside this house business, and I think I know what 'tis, but bes' I let her bring it up herself.'

"Mom," Sooky hesitantly said, "I guess I may as well tell you, Mr. Benson said he'd help us get the place. That is, he said he would room and board with us if it was alright with you. You know he likes your cooking, and that would give us the extra money we could count on even if our other work did slack off." She paused, then in a gush of words. "I just know we can 'swing it."

Mom chuckled before answering, "I knowed he wanted to help long time ago when he first started coming around. Jes thought to let you bring it up yourself. But, honey, yo' sho' that's all he want to do? Jes he'p? Don't go gittin' yo'self in no bind, trying to do better 'fore we able. We made out this far an' the good Lord'll help us further. We are gittin' more work, and things are better."

Sooky frowned and shook her head, "Mom, now there you go, trying to tie me up and read more into everything I say. You know I'm not untied from the other as yet. No, I'm sure he just wants to help, now, maybe later...." her voice trailed off. They sat in silence for a while before Sooky began explaining the rows of figures she was working on. The older woman nodded her head, sometimes in agreement, sometimes not. In the end, they were both in accord; they could swing it.

They discussed the move at length now, bringing up points in favor of it. The place had a chicken house, Mom pointed out, so maybe they could not only raise their own chickens and have eggs for themselves, but they might be able to sell a few. There was a good-sized garden space, and berry bushes were already planted. Sooky spoke of the large basement where clothes could be dried in inclement weather. There was also an ample space upstairs that could double as a play area for the children, or if their laundry progressed to that state, could be utilized for additional drying space. The neighbors all seemed friendly; the children would have playmates, and the new school was closer. The kids could play in the fenced yard. They would have room to stretch out, and so the talk went. Neither woman mentioned Mr. Benson further. Instinctively they both appeared to have come to the same unspoken conclusion; they'd cross that bridge when they came to it. Little did they know the reason they could swing it was because the house was between the homes of two families who were not, it seems, on the best of terms at the time. Friends of either family renting the house would have been embroiled in the vendetta. But, the house remained vacant for a more pertinent reason. The house was purportedly haunted! Hence the low reasonable rent. Since neither of these reasons were made known to Mom and Sooky, they were thankful for their good fortune of finding a suitable and reasonable house.

It was the kind of neighborhood whose relay system would rival anything the city folks or the outsiders would have for years to come. It was so near perfect that when the 'outside' authorities would make an unanticipated visit to check on the illegal 'joy-juice' making, the best they would find would be the pungent smell of the juice heavy in the air and the housewives busily and innocently making jelly or jam. The relay system worked. This was the new neighborhood. It was one step up, and things were getting better. The move brought perceptible changes to the family's way of life.

The floors were now carpeted, a few pieces of wicker furniture graced the front room, and crisp (carefully mended) curtains hung at the parlor windows. This was partly because some of Sooky's employers purchased new furnishings and gave her the cast-aways. The rest of the furniture had been procured by diligent searches of the second-hand stores and salvage stores.

The most important and welcome changes were the electricity and the inside plumbing. The flat irons and the kerosene lamps could now be put away. They weren't thrown away, oh no, Mom said, "Yo' nevah know when something might happen, and they come in handy." The big highlight was, they purchased the long-awaited electric washer (on credit, of course) with the help of Sooky's employers.

They were the first and only family in the neighborhood to have an electric washer for washing, which was only fit and proper. They were the first and only family in something else, too. They were surely the only ones who were not skilled in the art of making liquid refreshments such as wine, home-brew, or moonshine. They had to be taught, and prohibition was in force at that time. So, participation made life much less complicated and proved to your friends that you were not an outsider and could be trusted. After all, how could you rat on someone when you were doing the same thing?

The new neighborhood was not well-to-do or even middle class. Most men worked at the mills or did seasonal work (fishing, logging, etc.). The housewives did their own work. There was one or two families of American whites, several Italians, and a greater number of Slavic descendants with a sprinkling of Jewish families. Their family would also have the unquestionable honor of being the first and only Black family.

Precocious Brown Eyes

Oh yes, things were definitely getting better, but the chains of poverty still clanked loudly and showed no immediate signs of breaking. However, there was a slight possibility of a weakened link.

Mom was pleased to be of more financial help. She had her chickens and eggs now and found a ready market for all her surplus. Her cooking was indescribable, and Mr. Benson often carried a pan of rolls or bread into town to sell to some of his friends for her. Mom had the knack, possessed only by naturally bomb cooks, of making a gourmet meal of their simple fare. She could even turn the leftovers into something delicious. Cris would watch her take a pinch of this and a smidgen of that and turn a blah dish into a masterpiece. They ate well, and calories be hanged!!

Their laundry business was good too. One day, Mrs. Miller, whose laundry they did, asked Mom if she would mind working for her father. Mrs. Miller explained it was getting too much for her to care for her family and still have time to do what her father needed to be done. In the words of Mrs. Miller, "I just don't feel right taking so much of my time away from my family. I always feel like they must resent it. I do want things done for Daddy, but I just don't have the time. Now, I do want him cared for properly. He's such a dear and wouldn't complain no matter what or how things were done. Do you think you could do it?" Mom thought she could fit the bill.

The job paid well quite well until the daughter adjudged it was paying too well. She became positive her father was about to shower disgrace upon the heads of the blue-eyed members of her family, not to say bring to a halt the steady flow of cash that had been coming her way. Feeling that 'an ounce of prevention was worth a pound of cure,' she set about promptly and deviously to maneuver a romance between her father and an Anglo-American widow.

Mom relayed the events leading to the impromptu wedding; "Sooky, you know what I think Miz Miller think? She think her po' ol' daddy being too nice to me."

"Why do you think that? Did she say anything to you about it?" said Sooky.

"No, she ain't said a word to me about that, but, I noticed the las' two or three times I been there, she been coming by and generally stays 'til I leave. Guess she thinks I be spending too much time there." Mom said.

Sooky replied, "H'm. I thought she said she didn't have the time to be there so much on account of her other family. That was supposed to have been the reason she wanted someone to do for him."

"That's just it. She thinks somethin' goin' on wrong, cause, heah lately I been there mos' all day. Take las' week, fo' example, I cleaned the house and was all set to leave when he asked me if I would bake something for him to have on hand for snacking. I was in the kitchen with the door half-closed; I don't know where he was. He could have been out for a walk or gone to the store, but I know he'd gone out of the kitchen. Anyway, I heard the door open, and I thought he was coming back with something for the girls like he mos' always do when I'm there and getting ready to leave soon. I didn't go to see who it was 'til I heard those fas' footsteps, I know he didn't never walk that fas' so I stepped to the door to see who it be. I looked through the opening in the door, and there she was, jes' standing by his bedroom door like she was listening for something. She be so busy listening, she never did see me there in the doorway looking at her. When I spoke to her, she liked to jump outen her skin. You should have seen her face. She were reddem any beet," said Mom.

"What did she say?" Sooky asked.

"She grin like a fool and say she was going' shopping' and stopped by to see iffens her daddy want her to bring him something." Mom replied.

"Well, maybe she was," replied Sooky.

"Maybe she was is right. Soon as she find me there alone and him out and gone, she went right on back home herself. I know 'cause I stood right there and watched her. She didn't go near no store." Mom said.

"I suppose she does worry about him being there alone so much of the time. And, it was nice of her to want to go to the store for him even if she does call him to go for her most of the time. Guess she thought she would do something for him for a change since she couldn't spend time with him". Sooky chuckled.

"Well, iffen she gonna worry 'bout him she ought to worry 'bout the right things. Ain't nothing wrong with him 'ceptin' he mighty lonesome. That's why he has been asking me to cook something extra whenever I be there. He know that iffen I start to cook something' I havta stay 'til it's done. Mos' the time I'm trying' to cook, he sittin' there in my way jus' talking. The man jes' plain lonesome." said Mom.

"You could be right. How often has she come in like that?" Sooky replied.

"'Bout every time I go there here of late. Iffen she don't come, she send one of the kids up there. She sho' mus' not trust him or something. She jes' don't know me. She don' know iffen there was something goin' on. I'd done tol' her that I went long ago, back when she firs' started all that snoopin' around. For a while, it tickled me, but now it's plain makin' me mad. I can jes' see what was in her mind while she was standing at that bedroom door listening. She sure looked foolish when I called to her from the kitchen an' she found out he weren't even home or if he was he weren't in the house." Mom said.

Sooky laughed aloud at the mental picture she had of the event, then said, "She does have very funny ways. It seems she is not at all like most of the people around here. She acts like she thinks she is better than anyone else."

Mom said, "She don' know how close she came to getting a piece of my mind. I started to tell her, "I might have no husban' but I sho' ain't that bad off to have to be messin' aroun' with him. Mos' the time I cook, it's jes' so he can have some decent food to eat fo' a change, 'stead of that mess she was sending up there and callin' it food."

Whether or not anything was afoot, the dutiful daughter was taking no chances, and so the wedding took place shortly after that. What the good lady, in her self-righteous zeal to save her poor unsuspecting father from the clutches of a designing Black woman, didn't know or realize was, Mom was from the South and knew exactly her place in a bigoted society. What was more important was that she knew how to keep others in their places, too, if she felt the occasion warranted her use of such knowledge.

Mom welcomed the marriage because:
1. The new wife loved to entertain and did so frequently.
2. She liked a clean house and enjoyed good food.
3. Since her housekeeping and cooking left a lot to be desired, Mom was called in much more frequently.
4. The amount of laundry also increased. Thus the daughter unwittingly increased rather than decreased Mom's income. Oh,

the irony of her judgment. Both Mom and Sooky were working more outside the home and at home. The newly acquired luxury of electricity allowed them this privilege and gave them time for some social contacts.

Mom filled this newfound leisure time with quilting or sewing. Leisure time or not, she was not one to fritter away her time. Sometimes the older women would gather at one home or another to carry on these activities and have an evening of visiting and talking (gossiping). Mom enjoyed these times very much, as it had been a long time since she was afforded an opportunity of having contemporaries to chat with.

On these occasions, the respective hostess would show her delight and hospitality by providing her guests with some form of a repast. The refreshments would have been a connoisseur's delight! The borscht at one house; the cakes, the flaky pastries, fruit-filled delicacies, spaghetti, ravioli, fried chicken, cheese blitzes at another home. The list could be endless. In most houses, there was also the customary bottle of wine (home-made) or beer (home-brew) or maybe something even stronger. The reigning hostess would bring out her offering for the guests' enjoyment, each, it seemed, trying to outdo the former hostess. They would nibble and sip as they worked on their handiwork. This was usual for them, and they would urge Mom to join them in drinking a little something. Mom was not at all accustomed to drinking. True, she learned to make home-brew, but she didn't like the taste of it. Rarely would she indulge in a weak toddy or some egg-nog. So, the ladies would urge drinks on Mom, but she would only shift her snuff from one cheek to the other and shake her head in polite refusal. She should have kept it that way.

Chapter 5

It was a balmy evening. The children were happily and noisily playing; Sooky was home to watch them. Mom finished her regular daily chores and bathed. She hummed as she dressed. Maybe she would be able to finish the pillowslips she was currently working on tonight. She knew she was not interfering with any plans Sooky might have. Mr. Benson had already returned to town right after supper, so therefore he would not be asking Sooky to go out anyplace. Sooky immersed herself in a book. One could tell, just by looking at her, how much she missed her beloved books. So, Mom hummed contentedly, with a few grunts inserted when she tightened her corset strings. Mom was getting a bit plump and would not think of going out without being laced down. She often commented about stout women going without a proper corset or, at least, a firm girdle. She never admitted she was fat, just plump.

Her toilette was completed by touching a bit of color to her cheeks and darkening her scanty brows with a burned cork. She looked quite trim in her lavender flower-sprigged dress as she entered the parlor for Sooky's inspection. "Won't be gone too long. I jes' want to get this pattern straightened out. I 'hobbled' it somehow, she said as she departed. She walked primly out the door and down the steps pausing a moment to call to the playing children, "Don't you stay out here too long now. Go in before dark. Sooky be reading, and jes' might forget yo' out here". She hesitated, debating whether to go down the street and around the comer or take a shortcut through the break in the fence. The shortcut won. Seeing no one watching, she tucked her handwork under her arm, lifted her skirt slightly, and stepped nimbly through the break in the fence which separated the two houses.

From the opened windows came the sounds of shrill laughter and merry-making. The group was in a festive mood. Mrs. Angelo's daughter was going to have a baby! Her first grandchild! A drink or two was in order, they said. Mom thought it would be taken as an insult if she were to refuse at a time like this.

Mom's first drink seared her throat, assaulted her belly, and brought tears to her eyes, but that was the first drink. There were many toasts to be drunk. Long before the toasts were all drunk.... Mom was. She felt the urgent need for fresh air and struggled to her feet and made her way, unsteadily, to the door. The chatter and toasting continued undiminished, but then, someone was always going in or out. The air cleared her mind enough for her to know she should make 'tracks' for home.

She lurched across the yard, groped her way along the fence, searching desperately for the break she knew should be there. Someone must have moved it. It must have been nailed up since she had last used it. Eureka! She found it. She stepped through, not at all nimbly this time, almost falling and staggering around the house to crawl up the few steps. She was as sure as she could be in her condition; things would be alright if she once reached her bedroom and got to bed. She was so wrong. Oh, she got to bed alright, but......she was sick, SICK, and for the first and last time in her life, gloriously, hilariously drunk. Sooky put her to bed. Sooky and Jeanie chuckled for months over the amusing sight it was, but Cris was not content to just chuckle about it. Oh, no, not Cris, she had to mimic the performance and roar with laughter until a keen switch was applied vigorously to her long legs, which convinced her it might not have been quite so humorous after all.

Mom later said, "I don't know how in the world they can drink like that all the time, and it nevah seem to bother them. Thought my very insides was 'cornin' up. My head felt like it was split in two, and I think even my hair hurt. When I got myself straight, I promised the good Lord, I'd nevah do that again, as long as I lived. Magine me 'cornin' in 'fore the kids like that. I bound you, I'll nevah do it again." Mom would never say bet. She didn't believe in betting. Except for that enlightening episode, life was rather routine for Mom, Cooking, cleaning, and all the other tasks necessary to keep a household functioning.

Sooky was working quite steadily. She only had Sundays to look forward to for relaxation, and this was not always possible. There seemed to be some last-minute laundry or ironing left over to be done, no matter how hard they tried to get it out of the way before Sunday. They both believed Sunday should be a day of rest. As Mom put it, "Sunday is the Lord's day, or should be."

Each day Sooky would rise early to either begin or finish some chore at home before going to her job in town. Sooky was small and the embodiment of femininity. Even down on her knees scrubbing or waxing, her movements were fluid and somehow gave the illusion of daintiness.

To begin her long day, Sooky would have a light breakfast and dress for work. With her, everything had to be just so, no hanging slips or pinned straps. Her shoes must be polished, and the seams straight in her hose. Her work dress and apron were carefully folded and placed in a paper bag. She would never dream of working in the clothes she wore to work, and the idea of coming home in the clothes she worked in all day would have been extremely appalling to her. Some mornings Mr., Benson would claim he had to be in town early and would drop her off at work.

His early mornings seemed to coincide with hers quite frequently. It seemed since moving, Mr. Benson saw less of Sooky than when she was in the small cracker-box house. He was quick to grab any and all opportunities to be in her company or curry her favor.

Sooky was working so hard she had little time for social engagements, but she was determined the children would never have to work as she was now doing. She wanted to ensure them a better chance. It was hard denying herself so much, but at last, she was beginning to see the fruits of her labor. One of the first things Sooky indulged herself in was getting her beloved and much-missed books out of storage. Gradually she was improving her wardrobe, and so things went for a time, too long a time.

She was a good worker and well-liked by her employers. Some would say, with reluctance, "Sooky, I can't pay you what I should but, I have a friend who would be delighted to have you. She's quite well off, and you make her pay you well. I hate to see you leave me, but I feel guilty knowing you could be getting more pay and you do work hard." Sooky would then have a more lucrative job, but she didn't forget whoever was responsible for her good fortune, and whenever she had a few extra hours, she would work them in. In time, she was earning more in less time. The extra time at home was a welcome oasis in her drab life.

Now, some evenings she could go to a movie or have dinner out with Mr. Benson, and he was delighted. She could visit with the younger women of the neighborhood on some of her free evenings. They welcomed her into their circle with open arms, and they insisted she accompanies them to some of the local dances. They would incessantly chatter the latest romance, engagement, and all the things young, healthy, attractive women talk about. After leaving such a group, Sooky would feel more alive and exhilarated. Her step would be lighter and her laughter more infectious. "It's good to see," Mom said.

It wasn't until she was alone in bed when the disturbing, depressing thoughts came. It was then she would think of all the things she was missing. She loved to dance and was an extremely graceful dancer. She was young but realized she was fast becoming old by her secluded life. Finally, she capitulated to her minds' endless pleadings. She would go to one of the dances. She purchased the black patent high-heeled pumps (she preferred white, but black was more practical) and carefully chose a white eyelet dress with cap sleeves and a low perky flared skirt. Since it was summer, there was no need to buy a coat, for which she was thankful.

The big night arrived. She dressed with care despite the constant interruptions of Jeanie and Cris. Sooky always looked attractive when going out, but tonight there seemed to be an inner light behind her eyes. She was radiant. When, at last, she pirouetted before her mirror, in her whirly skirt and shining pumps, the girls were beside themselves with pride. She was not at all the same Sooky. She joined the group of girls at the corner, and away they went, chattering like magpies. Oh, it was good to be young and gay again. She had a wonderful time. It was not too difficult to persuade her the next time. It was at one of these gatherings that she met Kurt Sigma!

Sooky turned into the alley leading home. She was tired, dead tired and today had been especially trying. She would be glad to reach the refuge of her room. Her back ached, and she had cramps. The 'curse' was with her. She felt perfectly miserable if there was such a state of being and almost reached the back gate when she heard Marie calling excitedly to her. Marie lived next door and was the older sister of Tony. Sooky sighed and paused, waiting for Marie to catch up with her. Marie was in a dither. She was so flustered she was actually stuttering. Finally, she gathered her wits long enough for coherent speech. "Wilheim'll be home Friday," she gasped breathlessly.

Sooky smiled. She knew Marie had just cause for her near delirium. Wilheim was her fiancée. He fished for a living and was often gone for long periods of time, but now, he would be home Friday.

Marie rushed on, "His brother, Kurt is coming with him. I'm going to 'nail' him this time. He ain't going to get out on that boat again before I marry him. His brother's going to be best man."

Sooky congratulated her and they chatted briefly about the forthcoming wedding before Marie blurted out, "I wrote and told Wilheim about you, and he told his brother. Boy is his brother ever a good-looker. You'll like him, and I bet he 'goes' for you.

The last part of the conversation Sooky took as natural for Marie. They were close friends. Neither of them appeared to notice their ethnic differences. Before they parted, Marie extracted a promise from Sooky to attend the Saturday night dance and meet Kurt.

Sooky accompanied a bubbly Marie and a beaming Wilheim to the dance. They were both in high spirits, and the date definitely settled, but Sooky was a bit quiet and apprehensive. True, she always enjoyed herself at the dances and was anything but a wallflower, but then her dancing partners were all local neighbors. They accepted her as just another pretty girl, but how would Kurt react? He responded with courtly enthusiasm, and before the evening was over, the former dancing partners had the feeling they were too slow and lost out.

Kurt wasn't tall as men go, but he was quite a bit taller than Sooky. He had dark, almost black hair and sparkling deep blue eyes with sun and wind burned face. He was very good looking, and it was obvious he liked Sooky.

Sooky had no more free, lonesome evenings. Kurt saw to that, much to the dismay of Mr. Benson. Mom was non-committal about it. She appeared to have adopted a wait-and-see attitude. Being too young to realize the great impact this could have on their lives; the children were simply happy to see Sooky happy. Sooky's feelings fluctuated daily. Kurt was in there pitching.... and so was Mr. Benson.

Oh, Mr. Benson didn't fool himself. He knew he would have a 'tough row to hoe' to beat Kurt out; Kurt was younger, more handsome, and wealthier. The only tangible thing he could maybe count on as a mark against Kurt was that he was white (but Kurt apparently didn't know the difference in skin tones).

Mr. Benson didn't miss an opportunity to beau Sooky around, even if it meant taking the entire family. He became a strategist, devising, discarding, and revising plans only to dismiss them all as impractical and start all over again. Kurt accidentally supplied the key. Religion. That was it. Kurt was a strict Catholic. Mom and Sooky were Baptist.

Now, if he, Mr. Benson, could get them actively involved in the Baptist Church, he had it made. Whether 'Dame Fortune' was smiling on him or at him is a matter of opinion. Anyway, The Annual Convention was about to convene shortly, and he invited the ladies to attend. They met members of the Baptist faith and some very friendly, interesting, persuasive ladies from a Holiness church who extended them a cordial, sincere invitation to visit their church. More about that later.

Chapter 6

Jeanie was delighted with the new neighborhood. Now she had playmates her age, and, what was even better, Cris had playmates nearer her age. Now maybe Cris would not always be after her to read to her. (Dreamer, Cris still was after her and anyone else she could come over to read to her.)

When they could play without baby watching, they would choose teams for softball, play tag or hide and seek. Sometimes, though rarely, they would study together. The evenings were the best part of the day. The peals of spontaneous laughter would fill the air to express the joy of living. The groans of disappointment for a missed ball or a hiding place could be sensed as well.

When the boys were not around to play, the girls usually amused themselves playing hop-scotch, Red Rover, or jacks. Baseball and hide and seek were reserved as boy-girl games. School was fun; we competed and participated with our peers. Between learning 'The '3R's,' there were relay races, ball teams, and time just to play and tease. The playground contained many things, bars, swings, and other physical activities that were important for showing off. Jeanie would join the big kids for her trek to school, attempting to leave the little kids behind. The big kids tried all the tricks they could think of to accomplish this feat but rarely succeeded. On the few mornings, when they eluded the younger brother or sister, their victory would be brought crashing to defeat by an authoritative voice calling, "Jeanie, (Mary, Joe), wait for 'Baby,' (Tony, Benjy). You watch out for her." Dam little sisters and brothers!

In rainy or inclement weather, they would play in the basement at school. It was large and roomy, with seats along the walls. They would play simple games such as Red Rover. This was one of Jeanie's favorite games. To play this, they would choose sides before going to their respective places to stand facing the opposing team, holding the tightly clasped hand of the person next to them. The object of the game was for a member of one group to run and break through the line of the opposite team. Jeanie was always chosen first. She was built sturdily (chubby) and a speedy runner, a combination hard to beat in this game.

It had been raining and cold, so recess was to be in the basement. The two teams had been chosen, and Jeanie was called to challenge the opposers. She took a step back from her line to select a good spot to break through and spied two thin, lanky girls near the end of the opposite line. "They don't look like they can stop me," she thought and ran toward them. The girls knew their handholds would never stop this hurtling 'brown bomber' charging toward them and instinctively dropped hands. Alas, if Jeanie saw what happened, it was too late to change course, and her speed was too great to stop. She went through the line, all right, and smacked into the cement wall behind it. Oh, hoy, did she ever have a lump on her forehead. She was out, cold! She figuratively and literally knocked herself out! After that, Red Rover lost its charm for her.

In winter, Jeanie had to wear long-legged underwear (Union suits). Mom said it was a precautionary necessity to guard against pneumonia, arthritis, and many other ills too numerous to mention. Jeanie was aghast at the idea of the long, cumbersome underwear. She was positive they destroyed the shape of her legs, which was something to be proud of, and besides, none of the other kids had to wear them. She would leave home, all clothing intact, and, as soon as she was out of sight and could get the time to remedy the condition, she would immediately take them off, pull the 'long Johns' up and out of her stockings and tuck them inside the elastic bound legs of her panties. This maneuver took some time to accomplish. First, she had to lag behind the group, and secondly, she needed to make certain Cris was not around. When the deed was completed, she would have to run to arrive at school on time. The running was her jinx.

This particular morning it was harder than ever, practically impossible to get the privacy she needed to rearrange her clothing, but she did manage. She ran as fast as possible to arrive on time, but luck was against her. She was late. Everyone was in their seat when she breathlessly slipped in the door behind the blackboard, where the cloakroom was located to hang her wraps up. For a moment, there was silence, and then a ripple of giggles swept the room to become side-splitting, rib-tickling howls of laughter. "Don't see what's so funny about being late; lots of kids are late all the time," Jeanie mused. As she turned to leave the cloakroom, she looked down. She knew what was so funny. Clearly visible between the floor and the bottom of the blackboard was her underwear! The elastic failed her miserably! The legs of the underwear were down around her pretty legs in accordion-like folds! Jeanie fled to the Girl's room. The agony she suffered. She had a boyfriend in the room, and even he was laughing.

The new neighborhood opened up a whole new world for Cris. Now she was allowed to go to the stores with a note for Mr. Johnny at the market or Miss Katie at the general store, plus strict instructions about crossing the streets. She was going to school and was fast learning to read, not only the primary books of her class but also real, honest-to-goodness books. She was ecstatic.

Now she could find out what happened to "Sleeping Beauty" and 'Little Red Riding Hood" and so many, many more fictional characters who had become so very real and alive to her. While Cris was ecstatic about learning to read, Jeanie was deliriously happy to be freed from a Herculean task. Cris was a bookworm, alright, but that didn't interfere with her being one of the most mischievous kids in the neighborhood. Her boon companion, the boy next door, was the other one. They were inseparable pals. Cris and Tony fought daily but, woe betide any and all who tried to fight with either of them, They tramped the woods and beaches together and, between them, they knew all the best spots for a meeting-up and where most of the coach's moonshine were hidden. Sometimes, they would spend hours transferring a stockpile of bottles from their original hiding place to spots no poor unimaginative adult would or could possibly conceive. This pastime led, of course, to seeds of distrust springing up among the various owners of the contraband goods, and, not infrequently, the doubt exploded into blows.

When those two were on the loose, a clandestine meeting between the young lovers of the neighborhood was most apt to be virtually impossible. Those two small rapscallions imitated the lovers who so trustingly thought they were alone at the most inopportune times. Those kids weren't human. They were demoniac little imps!

Some days Cris and Tony would take their lunches and go berry picking to return heavily laden, juice stained, scratched, bedraggled, and full of grossly exaggerated accounts of the wonderful spots for berry picking they found. The mothers would promptly plan a berry-picking expedition for the next day, and Cris and Tony would be the official guides.

Precocious Brown Eyes

They wouldn't go straight to the area of the berries, not those two. They would crisscross, backtrack and wined around but eventually lead the older kids to their hidden treasure of berries. They had to do something constructive to validate their existence, didn't they? One day, in their ramblings, they discovered a large patch of huge blueberries. They weren't the kind of blueberries they knew, but the berries were large and blue. With all their combined woodlore, they were completely and absolutely stumped. They did the obvious. They scurried home to spread the news and, importantly, trekked back with their group of kids to pick the berries.

The kids picked and ate, as was usual, until buckets and stomachs full, they returned home. They were the typical young berry-pickers. They had juice-stained clothes, smeared faces, and blue tongues and teeth. Cris and Tony were comparably clean; they just watched the others.

The mothers took one look at the large blueberries and were petrified with horror. The berries were not blueberries. Oh, they were blue, alright, but no one knew what kind they really were. The neighborhood looked deserted for a few days. Cris and Tony wandered from house to house checking on the convalescing kids. Cris and Tony said, "Gee, they're all older than us and shoulda known better than to eat 'em," When the other kids did return to the streets, Cris and Tony stayed close to home, believe it or not where their parents could keep a watchful eye on them. 'Nuff' said.

Little by little, the neighborhood was changing. New people were moving in, and they were bringing with them a new atmosphere. Mom and Sooky knew what it meant. They recognized the symptoms but tried not to communicate their forebodings to the children, especially impressionable Cris. They calmly, gently but quite firmly and truthfully tried to prepare her by explaining to her the facts of life, not the sexual facts but the racial facts. She was duly warned some people were not as liberal as their old neighbors and was cautioned about the word 'Nigger' and its implication. But still, she was not wholly prepared. How do you prepare a little girl for a thing like that?

One day Cris was playing on the swings at school when Paul demanded she get off and let him swing. She refused and told him to wait his turn. His usually pale, freckled face darkened with rage as he glared at her. Then, he said it, "Nigger."

The other youngsters playing nearby fell silent. They all seemed to be staring at her. Cris felt her face bum. Her blood seemed to be boiling. As she let the swing's momentum slow to bring her near the ground, she valiantly tried to remember all that Sooky and Mom taught her. She looked at him standing there on wide planted feet in worn sneakers with his hands on his hips (he had no more hips than a snake). She looked at his scrawny frame, covered by faded jeans and an equally faded shirt, and thought, "even his eyes look faded." She remembered they said, "consider the source." They also said, "just ignore it." Cris was honestly trying and may have been successful if, for one thing, well, if he had gone away, but he didn't. Or, if he had not said more, but he did. He yelled out, "Black Nigger!" That did it! She forgot everything Mom and Sooky so painstakingly told her to do or not do. But, seeing the look on her face, Paul remembered what he was told to do, and he did it. He ran and hurried for the haven of the 'Boy's Room' with Cris hot on his heels. He escaped for the time.

He remembered to run, but he forgot that he sat in front of her in class and had an enormous boil on the back of his neck. Cris remembered all that and took action. She took her large

Geography book from her desk, took a healthy swing, and presto, an opened and well-draining boil plus a screaming Paul landed on the floor. The pain must have been excruciating.

Their teacher, Miss Randowe, was speechless and immobilized with surprise and astonishment for a moment. Then she dashed down the aisle to scoop Paul up in her arms and rush off to the First Aid Station. Cris calmly wiped her book and replaced it on her desk. Of course, she was promptly sent to the Principal's office and then home with a note for her parents. But she had been avenged.

That was the first real encounter with prejudice Cris experienced and, according to the standards set by Mom and Sooky, she failed miserably. Cris decided then and there it was due time she learned how to cope with the realities of life and do it her way. She had been reading and dreaming happily of being Sleeping Beauty or Cinderella, but the truth finally and irrevocably gotten through to her. She could never be like those story-book characters. They were all white! She put the fairy tales away along with the blonde, blue-eyed dolls and made her first step to change.

Chapter 7

In reality, things had been changing for some time, but Cris was too enraptured with her own little world to notice. The episode at school shattered the flimsy walls of innocence (ignorance), which she hid behind. If she had been more aware of things, she would have noticed other changes.

The boy-girl games were being played less. Now the boys would go off in groups leaving the girls to chatter and play alone. When they (the boys) decided to play with the girls, it was mostly teasing and hitting. A boy would snatch something from a girl and run or hide it behind his back or hold it over his head while she would try to retrieve it. There would be many giggles and playful wrestling with each other while the onlookers would teasingly urge them on. She also noticed it was usually the same boy-girl encounter.

Oh, they still descended upon the local movie house in force for the Saturday and Sunday matinee. They needed to know what happened to 'Pauline' (The Perils of Pauline), and no matter what was shown on the silver screen as happening to Pauline, it could never come up to the various conjectures they made during the week.

They were still a happy, boisterous group, but now, most of the older girls walked in a close cluster, chattering, giggling madly, and casting furtive glances at the boys behind them or milling around their group. Now and again, a bold lad would invade their ranks briefly, only to beat a hasty retreat by the jeering chant of his peers. "Joe's got a girl! Joe's got a girl!" Joe or Louie would chase the main offender and playfully knuckle him on the upper forearm or back, grinning idiotically. The girls would flutter around Joe's girl, like a bunch of butterflies, and ply her with questions. The girl, so singled out, would attempt to look important and demure but only succeeded in smirking foolishly.

Even Cris and Tony, "the inseparables," were not inseparable anymore. Tony would find his way off with the boys fishing or tree-house building, and Cris began to pester Mom more in the kitchen. Oh, they still found time to plot and carry out mischievous exploits together, but the breach was there.

Rarely, now, did they spend the long lazy days together, roaming the nook and crannies, free as the breeze, they had too much else to do. Mom guaranteed that. She said, "They gittin' too big to be off by themselves like that all day long." So, someway Sooky and Mom managed music lessons for the girls, and they were time-consuming. No matter what, Cris still found time to read. She read anything and everything printed that fell into her hands and, surprisingly, retained a great amount of what she read.

Cris read somewhere about reincarnation and was fascinated; the exotic bizarreness of the theory had a strong appeal for her. As a result of her avid reading about it, she incorporated its concepts into her storytelling. Some evenings, a group of the local youngsters would gather on the porch to listen, and she would hold them spell-bound with her tales. Here she was, one of the youngest of the bunch, and there they were, breathlessly caught up in her story and hanging on to each word as if their very lives depended on them. They would bombard her with questions of "then what happened?" or "How'd they do that?"

Sometimes Mom or Sooky would over-hear snatches of her stories and pause in their work to listen better. They were amazed at the skill and poise Cris possessed. No question seemed to rattle her. Her narratives were told so convincingly they had a ring of truth. In listening, it was hard to remember they were only figments of a childish imagination.

Mom and Sooky commented to each other about it. "Lord only knows how she can make up all them stories. Did you see those big kids sitting there listening just as if they believed her?"

"She's good, alright, but if she ain't careful, she gonna keep on telling them stories till she start believing them herself."

"Oh, all kids go through that storytelling period. They like to use their imagination."

"Yeah, guess they do, but I got a feeling her storytelling is more than just imagination. I think she really do believe in reincarnation."

When Cris didn't have a large audience, she could usually count on one listener, Jeanie. She could always capture Jeanie at bedtime if no other time.

Other changes were in the wind. The Saturday Matinees went on as before, but Sundays were different, oh, so different. Now they were up early to be combed, brushed, dressed, and redressed; checked and rechecked before departing for Sunday School in town. Here-to-fore, their attendance was sporadic as they had usually been able to beg off going if there was any local group activity afoot. Occasionally, Jeanie and Cris would accompany the neighbor youngsters to Mass. Cris loved it. She loved the pomp and ceremony; she loved it so well, it made Mom and Sooky do some serious thinking about the religious training for the children.

Sooky said, "When they don't go into town, they do go to Mass."

"Yeah, but they need to go to a regular Sunday School." Mom said.

"I guess it would be better. I know I always had to go when I was a child." Sooky replied.

Mom replied, "You shor did. I remember yo' was always at the head of yo' class."

"Oh, I don't know about that, but I did enjoy going," said Sooky.

"Then too, Jeanie gittin' up where she ought to have mo' friends of her own kind. These kids alright, but she needs to meet mo' of her kind, too," said Mom.

"She's got plenty of time for that. It comes soon enough. Anyway, things are changing. The color line doesn't mean as much now as it used to; it's breaking down," said Sooky.

"Yeah, it is, but I doubt if it will break in our time…or theirs either." Mom stated.

"No, it won't because we older ones won't let it." Sooky paused, deep in thought, then continued, 'You know, as much as we try to deny it, we have it too. It may be deep inside, it's true, but it's there." Mom didn't reply. She knew Sooky was not only thinking of the girls, but she was also thinking and trying to resolve her mixed feelings. She knew Sooky was fighting a battle of her own. She knew her mind was in turmoil, Kurt was pressing hard, but she also knew Sooky would have to work this problem out alone. Mom wisely did nothing.

What could she say? Sooky's words jarred a nerve she surmised was long dead. She had been away from the South for about 20 years. It was preposterous to think she still harbored the old way of biased thinking. But, did she? Wasn't that her real reason for insisting they join and attend the colored Baptist Church? On the other hand, hadn't she always taught the children and Sooky that color made no difference? Hadn't she always told the children, if people knew better, they would do better? But was she right?

She wondered if she was hypocritical; was she only mouthing words? But hadn't she accepted Kurt as a suitable suitor for Sooky? She knew Kurt adored the children and worshipped Sooky, as anyone with half an eye could plainly see. She welcomed the friendliness of all the neighbors and liked them all. Then, what was troubling her? Was she, as one of the older generation, unconsciously perpetuating prejudice? It was unthinkable, but she did some serious thinking, never-the-less. Mom wanted to be sure her concern was only to protect the children. She knew the snubs and slights of unthinking, uncaring people and the damage they could do. She had been through it and wanted to spare her children as much as was possible. Was it wrong to want to shield the children?

She realized she deviated from the big question. What kind of religious training for the children? Catholicism was not what she considered a suitable religion. It was too different from all she was taught, but it was better than none. They should attend a regular church. But to force the issue brought all these other facets into play. What decision to make and how to separate the facts needed a wiser head than hers.

Sooky was thinking, "It's really surprising. All these years, Mom has been teaching us not to judge a person by the color of their skin, and now, she's the one drawing the line!" Was it really better that way? To each his own? No, it's best to make your own choice. But, what choice was there if you only knew one side? What chance was there for a comparison? Maybe, it was best for the children to meet more of their own kind.

Mom said they should meet more of their kind. Did it mean she was secretly hiding her resentment and disapproval of her friendship with Kurt? Impossible! Mom liked Kurt, and anyway, Sooky remembered her father. He was as fair as Kurt, but he was Negro. Mom couldn't be prejudiced, or could she? No, that was unfair. Mom really liked Kurt, and no matter what else, she was not deceitful.

Sooky realized she had not been as fully or as long exposed to the extreme racial bigotry as Mom, so she consequently knew less and felt less about it. She did admit the late-comers to the neighborhood were not as open-minded as the old-timers, so Mom's way could be best.

Sooky was well aware of and equally disturbed by the lascivious stares directed at her when she and Kurt were together. Was that what she wanted for the children? Of course not! Things were changing, true, but bigotry was still very much alive. It wasn't fair to make a religious choice for the girls. The girls were growing up and should have a voice in the matter, too. But to do so, wisely, they would have to know both sides.

Maybe Mom was just lonesome and missed the many activities of the church. She had always been a good church worker. That was it. Mom was lonesome and felt neglected. She didn't understand what Catholicism meant and was much more familiar with the teachings of the Baptist faith. Sooky acknowledged that and felt that way at times. That had to be it, but was that all?

She knew they both wanted to do what was best and right for the girls. It didn't matter if there was a difference in opinions in how she and Mom saw things; they always agreed on one thing.

Do what was best for the children. But now, what was best? That was the big unanswered question!!!

The worrisome question hung heavy in the air and gave the women a sense of a rift between them. Nothing more was said about it for a while, but they felt the pressure of it building up and began to feel uncomfortable in each other's presence. The girls felt the tension too. It wasn't right or normal. Sooky and Mom had always been so close and open with each other. Each of the women was positive in her way of thinking. Now, could each of them be right? Would a compromise remove them from 'under the sword of Damocles?' Was it worth a try? No, compromising never solved anything. Compromising would just prolong it, but something had to be done. Their discussion ended with no resolution to the answer they were so desperately seeking. It seemed a vicious circle.

Mr. Benson accidentally supplied a part of the answer. One evening during dinner, he remarked that a vacancy in the Sunday School teaching staff was direly in need of being filled. It seemed one of the teachers had been called away due to illness in her family. He said he had taken the liberty of speaking to the Supervisor of Sooky's qualifications. He said he would be happy to make an appointment for Sooky to be interviewed if she was agreeable and would accept his intervention. The gesture surprised as well as pleased Sooky. Little did she dream of the selfish motive behind it. She did have her interview; as a result, she was accepted and agreed to teach as long as the regular teacher was absent.

Since Sooky was going to be teaching a class, she thought it only right that the girls attend Sunday School also, at least as long as she was teaching. Afterward, well, she would cross that bridge when she came to it. Thus, Jeanie and Cris were officially enrolled in The Baptist Sunday School.

Mom beamed contentedly; Jeanie was proud and pleased to meet new friends, but our Cris hated it all with all her heart, soul, and body. Sooky entered her teaching class with a great deal of trepidation. Even some of the girls in her class were larger than her, she felt very young and inexperienced, but she needn't worry. The young ladies of her class practically idolized her, and the young men, well, most of them had a crush on the pretty young teacher. She was an instantaneous hit, and She filled the niche perfectly. As her teaching assignment grew to a close, she began to wish, quite sincerely, that it was or could be a permanent thing. She was genuinely enjoying herself.

Sooky (and Mom) also realized she was in an excellent position to meet some eligible men of her own race. (Mr. Benson, in his zeal to remove her from the clutches of Kurt, hadn't counted on that). What better chance would she ever have to be able to test her feelings for Kurt? She knew he here-to-fore had no real competition. Ah yes, there was Mr. Benson, but that was just it; he remained just 'Mr. Benson'. He was nice enough, and Heaven knows he tried to change his status, but while she accepted and was grateful for his friendship, he remained, Mr. Benson, a dear loyal friend, and that was it. So, she continued the search for something or someone.

Mom was purring contentedly since Sooky was teaching, and she saw how nicely she fitted in. She was also satisfied to know the children were finally getting the proper teachings. Now it would be her turn to engage in some of the church activities. She hadn't admitted even to herself how sorely she missed the Sewing Circle, Missionary meetings, and all the other various events. Now she could fully and unrestrictedly indulge herself in them. The congregation welcomed her on the church dinner committees, and she was a wonderful cook. She was happy and busy doing the familiar things she knew, enjoyed doing, and understood. And Mom was pleased and content to have her little family participating also.

Jeanie rather enjoyed the change. She gloried in her new popularity. Most Sunday afternoons were now spent with some of the girls of her class. One or more of the girls would either return home with her to spend the afternoon, or she would accompany them to their homes. Her friends were from homes of varying economic ranges, and they also ran the full gamut of color tones. Jeanie was a democratic person.

Jeanie was a pretty child with deep dimples and a winsome smile which showed her small rice-like teeth. Her big luminous eyes were dark brown and had an engaging look of perpetual surprise or inquiry, while her hot-brown skin was as soft and flawless as rich velvet. Her hands were small and exquisitely formed, as were her feet and legs. She was lovable and loved being fussed over by the buxom matrons, and she also loved being the envy and admiration of the other children. Despite their obvious envy, she made numerous friends easily and quickly. She was accepted and received her new acquaintances without question. She was a lovely young girl.

Jennie's infectious laughter could often be heard in the baffled, beribboned group clustered around her. She always managed to look spick and span and very lady-like with her little white gloves and purse held just so. She was a natural coquette, even at her tender age, and all the young boys seemed to respond... hence, her popularity with the girls was intensified and strengthened. Contradictory reasoning? Not at all. It was simple and logical. Where Jeanie was or went. so went the boys, or they would surely soon be on the way.

Cris hated the many-hued, be-ruffled, and be-ribboned little girls. She hated the buxom matrons who were never satisfied unless they were hugging or patting some youngster. Why, oh why, couldn't they ever be content to speak? Why did they always have to touch you? Cris hated the physical contact, especially that of the fat, dark-skinned, sweating women. In fact, she had an intense aversion for dark skin, be it on young or old, fat or thin, male or female, be it dry or wet with perspiration. She just plain didn't like it at all. Cris knew it wasn't right for her to be that way because she had always been taught not to judge a person by the color of their skin. She knew it was wrong to pick friends by these criteria, but Cris wouldn't or couldn't bring herself to do otherwise. She couldn't repress the feeling of repugnance for black skin.

She knew better than rebuff the darker youngsters openly because it would bring disaster in one fell swoop to let her repugnance show with the adults. As of now, she didn't have much choice of the youngsters she was forced to be around, but she certainly, by hook or crook, was going to eliminate the real dark ones. With this goal in mind, Cris launched herself on the way to selectively choose her friends. Little did she know at the time how she was going to accomplish this feat and how to get past Mom's watching eye. She was searching for and selecting her kind of people.

Cris was not a demonstrative person, not even with her own family. She was really shy, and any overt display of affection embarrassed her. Her shyness was quite misleading. People thought she was timid, but she was anything but timid. Her shyness was motivated by aloofness. When they would arrive at the church and alight from Mr. Benson's car, Cris would always take a deep breath of fresh air before entering. It always seemed to be hot and stuffy inside, no matter what the weather. The church continually smelled of cheap perfumes and powders to her, vainly trying to compensate for unwashed bodies. They wore strong hair pomades too. Cris would mentally wrinkle her slightly flattened nose preparatory to enter and endure her time of confinement inside.

She became quite adept at evading unwelcome embraces. If she saw one of the ladies bearing down on her, she would suddenly remember a forgotten article in Mr. Benson's car or hear a nonexistent voice calling to her, and away she would dart. However, she would first curtsy prettily and make her excuse, that is, if she thought she had that much time. Or if her 'enemy' was too close for the show of politeness, she would simply dart off then stop abruptly at a safe distance, to curtsy and make her excuse to the dear lady. Cris was small and slender and could move with animal grace and cunning.

The ladies were delighted by her manners and commented on her impeccable politeness. They were thoroughly intrigued by her quaint, old-fashioned curtsy and thought it was sweet and considerate. Cris didn't give a fig if it were polite, sweet, or considerate. She did it because it usually gave her time to escape their embraces while remaining in the good grace of Mom or Sooky. Cris did it (the curtsy) for another reason; it gave her a chance to show off her long thick braids. She knew when she bowed (she practiced in front of the mirror enough), her braids would swing forward like big coils of rope. Oh, she was proud of her hair. Cris knew she wasn't a pretty child by any stretch of the imagination. Her face was too thin, and her large almond-shaped eyes overshadowed it. Her mouth was quite generous, and her nose was too flat. No, Cris knew she was no beauty. She didn't smile much because of a gap in her front teeth, but she knew she could let her eyes express what she wanted people to see and think. Never once did anyone guess that while she looked like the picture of innocence and sweetness, her mind was busily plotting and planning, sometimes (most times) not at all innocently.

Chapter 8

While the rest of the family was busy enjoying the camaraderie of their new acquaintances, Cris was busily engaged in cataloging and classifying her new friends. She was selective and confident beyond a shadow of a doubt that she was doing it with such finesse and skill that no one realized it. True, she hadn't much choice of the youngsters she was forced into contact with, but Cris certainly intended to make her own choice of those she was to be friendly with. Her friends had to meet her fixed and rigid particular criteria. The criteria were color, appearance, financial standing (why bother to cultivate a friendship with someone poorer than you?), and home environment. They were judged in that order.

The color requirement was determined simply and adeptly by a thin arm or leg (her own) surreptitiously beside the candidates. An artist couldn't have chosen hues truer to the original 'yardstick.' None of her friends were too pretty. Cris did not like to be in too much competition and was honest about her appearance. The financial standard was the most flexible. It only required that the youngster pay their way unless Cris was in one of her rare charitable moods. The home environment was another of the inflexible musts. The people living there had to be clean and not smelly as well as their house. To her, no one was clean who had greasy plastered down hair or kinky hair.

Jeanie was constantly going off with her friends or having some of them spend time with her. Cris usually stayed on the sidelines wondering why Jeanie couldn't be more discriminating in Heaven's name? There were few homes she would visit and fewer friends she would invite to come to her home.

Sometimes, the whole family would be invited to dinner at a home, which should have been taboo to Cris. On these occasions, she would wonder how Mom and Sooky could or would want to develop any friendship with the family. She would look appraisingly at the adults. Most of the time, it would be a perspiring man in a too snug collar with rolls of fat overlapping it and one who appeared ill at ease and quite uncomfortable in his Sunday best. Most of the men wore their hair two different ways. It was either so kinky as to appear uncombable or so slicked down with grease as to look like it was lacquered. The women were usually fat, flabby, and misshapen, reeking of Mavis Bath Powder and Evening in Paris perfume. Cris would compare Mom and Sooky to her hostess and inwardly shudder at the comparison. She guessed both Mom and Sooky perspired, but if they did, it was never to the degree of those large wet, discolored, smelly underarm circles these women did, and Mom was as corpulent as some of the other women. Somehow, Mom and Sooky always looked fresh, and what was more important to her was that they always smelled fresh, so why couldn't these other women?

Most of the parents usually had dark, ashy-faced children or children so oiled that they shone like polished ebony. Either way, Cris found them repulsive but found a believable and legitimate way of not joining them in play. She would resort to sticking a long thin finger down her throat to induce vomiting. Sometimes this subterfuge was unnecessary. Merely watching them gulp their food so voraciously would nauseate her.

On the Sundays Cris was invited out for an afternoon by an unacceptable prospective hostess, she would politely turn them down with the pretext of unfinished school work. Since she was an excellent student, this excuse was usually accepted. Sighing with relief at her narrow escape, Cris would search her brain for anything she could do for extra schoolwork. Was it any wonder she was an honor student? Her study period at these times would vary according to what activity she wished to participate in. If Sooky and Kurt were planning to go for a drive, the schoolwork was swiftly disposed of. Since neither of them could refuse her silent wistful plea, she usually accompanied them. On the other hand, this study period was unfailingly long if work was to be done at home. Long enough anyway for the work to be completed or almost completed before she was free to offer her services.

Although she and Jeanie were sisters, they were in no way alike. Jeanie was open and friendly, while Cris was just Cris. Mom and Sooky often commented about the difference in their personalities. They would say, "Those two are as different as day and night." Their lives may have turned out a lot different if only Mom and Sooky had been content to just stay at the Baptist church. Cris thought she might have come to like it in time, but no, Mom and Sooky had to meet some "Holiness" members and go traipsing off to the Holiness Church. "Just visiting," they said.

Mom said it reminded her of the Apostolic Church back home. Sooky was non-committal about it on their first visit. Jeanie was wide-eyed, and Cris was crestfallen by the evident poverty of the place. Why it was worse than the little brown cracker-box house, they lived in. She was furious at Mr. Benson for being so kind and good as to take them there. She was too young to understand Mr. Benson would have taken them to the ends of the earth, if possible, had Sooky expressed a desire to go there and he was permitted to take her.

There were no rugs on the floor unless you call the moth-eaten threadbare one in front of the makeshift pulpit. The pews were a little better than rough planks nailed together. The only good feature Cris could see was the place did have windows. The first time they visited this Church, Cris fervently hoped throughout the service it would be the last. These people looked worse than the others.

The visits became more and more frequent until, eventually, they went regularly. The singing and the music were foreign to Jeanie and Cris. They were accustomed to the more sedate formal services of the churches they formerly attended. Here, the choir was drowned out almost by the piano, guitars, and the tambourines wielded by sweating, madly gyrating, shouting congregation members. They never seen or heard anything like it.

Cris would wriggle uncomfortably on the rough bench, careful not to get a splinter in an embarrassing spot of her scanty posterior. She was grateful Mom and Sooky were not a part of this hysterical group. Alas, her gratitude was short-lived. Mom and Sooky both joined, or, as the new church taught, were 'reborn' or 'saved.' Cris wondered, 'saved' from what? They looked the same to her, and they still lived and worked like always. So, what was all the big hullabaloo about? The only tangible thing she could notice was, Mom stopped dipping snuff, and she and Sooky quit making home-brew.

The cessation of the beer-making shook became tranquil to Jeanie. Jeanie loved the taste of home-brew and would often (well, as often as she could manage) get a bit tipsy by furtively sneaking down in the basement and drinking from the spigot of the beer barrel.

Well, the beer was poured out, and Cris was delegated to throw away and hide Mom's snuff. Her reason being, Mom, said before she was quitting that they (Sooky, Jeanie, and Cris) ended up walking a mile or so to the drugstore to get her another jar of snuff. This wouldn't happen this time, Cris vowed, so she just hid it. Now, when Mom expressed a desire for her snuff, Cris would be able to deliver without the fuss and bother of going all the way to the drugstore. She congratulated herself on the foresight, but Mom never asked for snuff again from the night she was 'saved.'

Cris was disappointed her precautionary effort had gone to waste and consoled herself with the thought of no more long trips to the drugstore.

She didn't like to go to the store because they had to pass a house where a big yellow dog was kept. This darn dog would jump up on the fence (it looked frail to Cris), barking and snarling viciously. Cris always feared he would break out, and she was frightened of dogs, large or small. All that was needed for her to break out with nervous perspiration was to ascertain it was a dog!

As well as not having to trek to the drugstore for snuff for Mom, they were no longer allowed to trek to the Saturday and Sunday Matinee. Movies were considered against the teachings of the new church. Cris was beginning to see what they were 'saved' from. As most new converts were apt to do, they didn't miss a service. This in itself wouldn't have been so bad, but the services were abnormally long. The girls would nod during the long-winded testimonies and drawn-out sermons, wishing they were home in bed. The lengthy services and all the new teachings produced still other problems aside from two sleepy children.

Mom and Sooky, in their zeal not to miss a service decided they lived too far from the church. It took too much time to get there, and the transportation was uncertain if Mr. Benson was unable to accommodate them. So, another change was about to take place. The house in town was no improvement over the one they left. Mom and Sooky acted as if they thought this was another step up. The only difference was it was closer to the church and some cheaper shopping stores. Some of the places Sooky worked were not within walking distance. That was all that Cris could see.

They said their goodbyes with many regrets to the old friends and neighbors. These people became very close and dear. Mr. Johnny at the market was always so good. He never sent the wrong cut of meat and always remembered Mom liked liver sliced thick, no round bones in the pork steak, a streak of fat, and a streak of lean in the salt pork. She didn't like salt pork real fat. He never sent them a bill and trusted them to pay when they had the money. Mom and Sooky never once betrayed that trust. There was Miss Mary at the general store. She always told Mom whenever she had a bargain in the dry goods department. Some of the goods were discontinued; Mom and Sooky got a good bargain price. Sometimes, the reduced prices would coincide with things she knew or felt the family needed or wanted.

Even now, as they were loading the truck, with the help of the closest neighbors, others were coming to offer help and bring various-sized mysterious packages.

The neighbors said, "Jussa lil' bread. You always saying how you like this bread."

"Ma sent these sausages. She said you don't have to cook 'em. They're all cooked. Ya kin have them for supper."

"Sornma cheese. Taste good with coffee and bread. This you can't get in town. My family maka this kind for a long time."

And so, they came. Some left with just a hearty handshake but most embraced the women, and with terse commands for them to return and visit, they returned to their home. Some were visibly crying. Others elected to remain to help with the work.

Overall was the shadow of sadness. All felt a keen sense of loss. The women, for the good kind neighbors and the neighbors, for this remarkable family.

Thus, they said their farewell to this old neighborhood and promised many friends a return to visit and keep in touch. They were warned they wouldn't like living in town and were urged to move back if things didn't work out well for them in town. The neighbors were reluctant to let them go. They had come to love and respect this 'black' family, and their love for them had completely erased the color. The family had become just another family in the neighborhood.

The truck was finally loaded, and the family departed amid much shouting and a flurry of waving. Mr. Benson and Kurt, for once, worked together side by side. Mr. Benson transported the girls and Mom. Sooky elected to ride with Kurt on the truck.

All in all, Mr. Benson had taken their decision to move with extreme good grace, considering the decision also omitted him from the new household. Since joining the new church, Mom and Sooky deemed it unsuitable to have a single male roomer. So, he chose with all the circumspect lodgings nearby. At least he would live closer than Kurt, and he would certainly attend that church and be available for transportation whenever they (Sooky) desired.

Mom and Sooky realized the children would sorely miss the old familiar surroundings and friends, but they would soon adjust as children. They would meet new ones and have more opportunities in town. Sooky would be closer to her work. Mom knew she would miss her garden and chickens but felt she could probably busy herself with the myriad church diversions. Sooky seemed to be taking the move better than any of them. She appeared more at peace with herself than she had been in a long time.

The new neighborhood residents were curious about the newcomers, and many window curtains were constantly adjusted to accommodate the discreetly peering occupants of the neighboring homes. Mr. Benson and his passengers arrived first, causing hardly a stir, but when Sooky and Kurt arrived, wow! Prudence and discretion flew out of the window. They stared openly and flagrantly. Another 'black' family in the neighborhood was bad enough, but a mixed household was entirely too much. It was simply unthinkable. That would be entirely too much to take!! What was the neighborhood coming to? Disgraceful! Outrageous!.

However, their fears were needless, for when the truck was unloaded and the heavier furniture placed, Kurt departed.

Chapter 9

So they were nearer the church and were plunged headfirst into all the church bustle. On Sundays, the schedule was,

(1) Sunday School,
(2) Morning worship
(3) Bible Study,
(4) Evening Service.

Then there were other church services or activities scattered throughout the week. It seemed to the children that there was always something going on at the church. Then there was the Prayer Meeting and special programs, you just name it, and you had it. They didn't miss a one. The children might yawn, nap, grumble and frown, but attend they did.

For a time, the household was evenly divided. Mom and Sooky 'saved' — Jeanie and Cris 'unsaved.' At first, the girls were allowed to participate in some games and amuse themselves to some degree, as other youngsters did, but as Mom and Sooky grew in the church's doctrine, they became stricter on the girls. One by one, their so-called worldly pleasures were eliminated. It was a sin to play cards and ball, even for fun. It was a sin to play the old records, although the girls played them whenever their parents were not around. It was a sin to dance, but both the girls knew how to dance most of the latest dances; they could not dance openly. According to what they were being taught, almost anything that was any fun was a sin. If there had been any question in the mind of the girls what being 'saved' meant, it was now fully answered. It meant being kept from any fun.

Fortunately, most of the members had children near the ages of Cris and Jeanie. The youngsters would all sit in the back of the church and giggle and smirk at their parents' antics and other adults until they were caught. The offender would be called by a nod or a look of the parent and made to sit with them for the rest of the service.

That's the spot Cris usually found herself occupying. For some reason, she couldn't control her joy. She let her imagination run and would compare the sweating, shouting adult to the various animals she would think of and draw caricatures of them which she would pass out to the other youngsters, hence the fits of giggling in the back of the church.

Gradually the number of 'unsaved' youngsters was getting smaller, while the Jr. Choir of 'saved' youngsters grew larger. It seemed most of the kids had just given up and followed in the footsteps of their elders and joined the church. Frankly, they didn't have another choice. They may as well join since they were cut off from most of the enjoyments other normal children enjoyed. Cris thought, "Well, let them all join. Jeanie and I won't!" Then the bottom of her dreams fell out. Jeanie capitulated and went over to the enemy! Jeanie joined! She couldn't – know, she wouldn't - but - she did. Jeanie was now a member of the Jr. Choir too.

Cris was flabbergasted. What was she to do now? She felt completely alone. "O. K." she mused, "If you can't beat 'em, join 'em." She knew she couldn't beat all of them. Jeanie maybe if given time, but Sooky and Mom, never. There was nothing else left to do but join. Her joining performance should have been awarded an Oscar. It would have taught even Barrymore a few new twists. The naive oldsters in the church had never seen the likeness of it and were jubilant. Just think, a complete family 'saved.' It was just wonderful.

Cris had finally made up her mind to join after she was, in her opinion, singled out to be preached to. Of late, most of the sermons seemed to be centered on one single subject. "Suffer the little children to come unto Me." Since she reasoned she was about the only little child left who was near old enough to have any idea of what it was all about, this had to mean her. So, she made her way meekly to the alter, along with the other repentant sinners, to kneel before the rough 'mourners bench.' Despite the loud singing and tambourine banging, she bowed her head on her small, folded hands and promptly fell asleep. A hand placed on her head awakened her. She wondered how long she slept. She peered cautiously through her clasped fingers along the length of the now-empty bench and thought, "O, boy, I've gotta do something now. I can't afford to let them know I went to sleep, so here goes." She did something alright; she watched the other converts long enough to know what was expected.

Cris flung her thin arms high overhead and let her eyes roll wildly. She fell over backward on the floor for the grand finale and began to roll recklessly and vigorously about while uttering gibberish sounds. The sounds were in answer to the many screams of "that's it!" "She's got it!" It was a true command performance. The likes of which had never been seen before or thankfully since. Her performance didn't win her a place in the Hall of Fame; it did (due to her nap) win an extra day of rest from school for her and Jeanie.

Their family was a welcome addition indeed to the small congregation. Both women would work diligently on the various committees, and Mom's dinners could not be beaten or even equaled. Sooky brought a new freshness and grace into the otherwise drab surroundings with her cheerfulness and poise. There weren't many young, attractive female members, and the Deacon board members were still very much male and let no one tell you any different. They welcomed Sooky, and their attendance showed a remarkable increase and improvement.

The family hadn't been members very long when the time came for the Annual Baptism rolled around. As new converts, they were asked (urged) to be baptized. They declined by reason of a prior baptism. Cris watched the ritual with keen interest. This was completely new and different from anything she had ever seen before. The baptismal candidates were lined on the shore of the lake where the event was to take place. The women were all dressed in white, and their hair was carefully tucked under rubber swim caps. Baptism or no, they were not about to let their hair get wet under any conditions. No siree. Not them. Most of the male candidates were coatless, and their white starched shirts gleamed in the bright sunlight. There were two tents set up close by the water to be used as dressing rooms. A short distance away, the picnic tables were laden with white dishcloth-covered baskets. Indeed, this proved to be the best part of the day for the children. They found it quite hard to wait for the last candidate to be baptized, and the service to end so that the women would be free to start spreading the contents of the many baskets.

The day would end in feasting and singing. It was a wonderful experience for Cris. She wished it would never end. Due to the gentle yet constant pressures, the women relented in their decision during the following year. The next time they and the girls would be baptized. After all, the girls had not been baptized before, and as Mom put it, "Wouldn't hurt me and Sooky none at all to be redipped."

The coming event enchanted Cris. She planned precisely how she would behave. She imagined and pictured how to walk daintily out into the water to the waiting minister to be dipped under the lake's rippling blue surface. And then, she would emerge triumphantly and gracefully to make her way proudly, yet with dignity, back to the waiting crowd on the beach. Oh, she was going to be magnificent. She would even consent to be hugged and kissed (yuk) by some of the ladies. (That's what she had seen, them do to the others last year). She would let them protectively wrap her in a blanket and escort her to the 'Ladies tent' to be dried and redressed before she sweetly and saintly rejoined the singing group at the water's edge, watching the remainder of the convert's baptism. She had it all so beautifully planned in her mind.

What actually happened was that Cris could only take a few steps into the water before it was too deep for her to walk, so she was carried out to the minister by the two stalwart deacons. The water of the lake wasn't a beautiful blue; it was a sickly greenish-brown. She was dipped under as planned, but she didn't emerge gracefully. She came up sputtering and kicking wildly. Pride, dignity, triumph, and grace were all forgotten in her haste to get her feet back on solid ground. As far as her sweet, saintly onlooking at the water's edge was concerned, Cris couldn't have cared less. Her only concern was that she was dry and warm again. That water had been cold. Ah, the folly of her imagination. The girls were growing up in the church, but Cris always felt like an outsider. Surely these people were not her kind, and she must look further.

She certainly didn't want to be like most women or men she met there when she was grown. For example, Sister Wishman towered over most of the other women and made Sooky look dwarfed. Sister Wishman had relatively coarse features and was built as solidly as the Rock of Gibraltar. Sister Wishman (all the women were either called 'Sister' or 'Mother') was always around the younger women, busily teaching them the church's doctrine. This took so much time she didn't have any time to instruct the older women. If Cris had been more schooled in the ways of life and the many facets of it, she would have recognized Sister Wishman for what she was.

Then there was Sister James; she was the church matchmaker and troublemaker. Her meddlesomeness usually turned out to be big trouble. She was tall, angular, and black with a 'horsey' face. She could talk more and faster while spraying the air and anyone in the vicinity with spit. Sister James made up her mind that Kurt was not the one for Sooky, nor Mr. Benson either. Not either of them, but now, Deacon Sayles was just the man. He was a marvelous catch, according to her. Cris wondered why, in heaven's name, if he was such a wonderfully great prospect, Sister James or someone else wasn't trying to catch him? To Cris, Deacon Sayles looked like a great lumbering grizzly bear. He pushed himself around in his shiny blue serge suit and his bald yet shiny bullet-shaped head. He domineered the rest of the deacons. He would grin foolishly and lustfully whenever he could see Sooky for a few brief words. Cris would shake her head dolefully. Surely Sooky could do better than that!

Then there was that young minister, Elder Fordabar. He was the most conceited male she had ever seen. He was sure he was God's gift to women. He always contrived to be behind the shapelier women when they were ascending the stairs. He devised ways to be able to pass the younger women and girls in close spaces so he would be forced to press against them in passing. However, he had a wife, but that fact didn't deter him in the least. It only made him more cunning and sly.

    The length of undesirables was or would be too long to mention all. But, there were some gems scattered amongst the people. Sister Walter was about the sweetest person anyone could ever meet. To be counted among her friends was a privilege. Her understanding and wisdom appeared boundless. Cris adored her almost as much as her own family. Deacon Lodge and his wife were, to Cris, the ideal couple. Sister Lodge was small and dainty, while he was so large and masculine. Mrs. Lodge was how she imagined Sooky would be when she reached that age. Deacon Tyne and his wife and a few more met the requirements of Cris, but on the whole, these were definitely not her kind. Cris would sit and listen to Elder Ernest, the pastor, pleadingly implore his flock to faithfully and prayerfully read their Bibles and to live according to the teachings therein. He would preach, tears intermingled with sweat rolling down his face, to the point of exhaustion. Entreating his congregation to let 'the beauty of Jesus be seen in them'; 'to live in the world but not of the world'; 'to let their light shine.' That man could really preach. He made you believe he believed what he preached, and Cris wondered if he lived what he preached.

    Cris would sit and listen to his voice which was sometimes low and sad, and at times, vibrant with emotion. The audience would sometimes echo his mood with a low mournful lamentation or exultant shouts. When he stood, with arms up-praised in benediction, Cris thought Jesus might have appeared this way when He stilled the waters of Galilee. She imagined if Christ had ever been portrayed as a black man, He would have looked like this man.

The adults said Elder Ernest's wife was the 'helpmeet' the Bible spoke of. She had the face of an angel, serene, calm, and beautiful. Not beauty as beauty is generally thought of but an inner beauty only a person who has found the ultimate contentment possesses. They were the perfect couple and entirely devoted to this small church and each other, but, most of all, to God. They were uniquely wonderful. Never once did you hear a word or see a look of reproach at a too meager offering. God was thanked as reverently for the pennies and nickels as for the rare greenbacks. They never voiced a complaint about the sometimes empty cupboard. They had to believe, "Man does not live by bread alone." Or else they could never have survived this long. Mom's abundant Sunday dinners helped to bridge the gap.

Cris would scan the congregation's faces, watching the impact of Elder Ernest's words on the people listening to him. Most would look transfixed, hanging on to his every utterance. She would look at Mom and Sooky; Mom would be completely entranced. At times Sooky's face seemed to be lit by an inner glow. Cris would not have been too surprised to have seen a halo above her head.

On rare occasions, Kurt would venture to attend a service; she watched his reactions closely. Sometimes his face wore a puzzled, perplexed expression. At other times a faint frown would crease his brow, and at still other times, a faraway dreamy look would steal across his face. He would look at Sooky with love and longing. Cris ached for him and yearned to know how to help him through this maze of religious barriers and to Sooky. She didn't know how or where to begin or even if there was a way. Somehow, she sensed, in some way, that more walls were being put up. Cris would even pray silently, "Dear Lord, help them to find a way." She didn't feel sacrilegious, only uttering her pleas for help, not only to bring happiness to two of the few people she was fond of but also mostly for herself. Sooky worked so hard to provide the necessities for them, and now, if only a way could be found for her to marry Kurt, things would be so much easier. Not only would Sooky have a husband, but she wouldn't have to work as she did. This was important to Cris, and their family would have a father like most of the other youngsters. It would, in her estimation, raise her prestige considerably. And, so she prayed earnestly, "Dear Lord, help them find a way."

Cris would shift her gaze from the adults to the members of the Jr. Choir. Some of them (the kids) seemed to dig this cloistered, secluded way of life, but most chafed under the restrictions it placed on them. She often wondered if this way of living was only acceptable to people who had lived more of life. People who had become tired and jaded, those looking for something new and different. But these kids never had a chance to know life, much less a choice of what they wished to make of it or how they wanted to live it. It was unfair. Often, under the watchful eyes of their parents, they were beautiful examples of 'God-fearing, God Loving' youngsters, but it was usually a case of out of sight, out of mind, or when the cat's away; the mice will play and play they did.

She knew it was wrong to pretend. Most of the kids, including her and Jeanie, did everything any other youngster did. Most of them didn't have strong enough convictions to be different from the other kids, so they were hypocrites. Oh, they weren't hypocrites by choice because they were weak, too weak to admit to doting proud parents that they couldn't cut the mustard. They weren't strong enough to withstand the anguish or the humiliation it would cause their parents to admit to 'backsliding,' and so they lived dual lives.

Chapter 10

As the girls (Jeanie and Cris) grew into their teens, they became more and more determined to make decisions for themselves. They became a lot more critical and observant; they could see the human failings and imperfections and found the courage to 'back-slide.' Cris never learned the source of Jeanie's courage. Maybe it was biological. She had grown to be a very pretty girl with a marvelous figure. Perhaps it was the newly awakened awareness of the opposite sex. No matter what the source, she found the courage. The courage needed to be honest with God, her parents, and herself.

Cris knew where her courage came from. It was due to an all-consuming hatred for Sisters Wishman and James. Those two, for some unknown reason, zeroed in on Sooky and were wearing her down. They claimed to be having dreams, visions, and messages given to them from the Lord, denoting His will for Sooky to marry that bullet-headed, clumsy, blunderbuss Deacon Sayles. Since it concerned Sooky, should those two be the ones to whom the messages and visions were given? Why not to Sooky herself? Wasn't it all just a lot of hocus-pocus because they didn't approve of Kurt? Why couldn't Sooky see what they were trying to do?

Boy, Deacon Sayles must really be paying them off well to plead his cause so eloquently. Oh, not paying directly, of course. That would have been unthinkable to the good ladies but by donating substantial sums to their various projects in the church. Mom didn't seem to see what was going on at this time.

The church seemed to have numerous occasions for fellowshipping that always culminated in big dinners. Of course,

Mom was always called upon to coordinate these meals. She would always seem to do most of the preparing and would bring at least one or more of her special dishes. Unbeknownst to her, she was rapidly winning the admiration and adoration of a widower in the congregation. If it is true the way to a man's heart is through his stomach, then Mom had an eight-lane highway to Deacon Bartles' heart. He was not even a member of that particular church at first but saw Mom and tasted her food at one of the fellowship dinners.

After that, he made all the rest of the dinners and soon became a frequent Sunday guest at the family's home. He had been widowed for five years after a very long and happy marriage. His adult children lived elsewhere and didn't keep in close contact with him. In a short time, he asked Mom to marry him. Mom hesitated a bit but was encouraged by Sooky (who was still trying to sort out her feelings about Kurt). The girls didn't know what to think until Deacon Bartles began playing them with small gifts and assured them he wanted to become part of the family and had no intentions of breaking it up. Things began to be easier for them all.

"Dad," as he soon became, put enough money into the home to allow Mom to give up all outside work and concentrate on the family. They always had a clean home and good food. Now, Mom did more baking and entertaining their friends, and Sooky was able to relax a little and not worry so much about making ends meet. She could even spend a little more money on the girls. Things might have been near perfect had it not been for those two particular sisters at the church. Why couldn't Sooky do as Mom had done? Mom met and married a man of her own choice without all the visions and messages. Sooky was entirely too sweet and gentle to fight these two old war-horses. She didn't know how to begin. Maybe it was because of her upbringing, "respect and obey your elders." Phooey!!! Sisters Wishman and James had been around a long time and in a lot of places.

They knew the ropes and all the angles. They argued Deacon Sayles' good points. He was a deacon in the church, and he was employed. He owned his own home, which would be so good for the girls. Hog-wash!! He had a run-down house that seemed like it was in the middle of a marsh when it rained, and it was surrounded by parched, weed-choked brown grass in the summer. The only thing Cris could see that he had going for him was his two emissaries. And, since they were getting all the visions and messages, maybe one of them should have him. They seemed to think he was such a great catch; they should be the ones to catch him. In the end, they finally wore Sooky down. It was all settled. All that was left to do was to tell Kurt of their decision.

Cris would have given her left arm to have heard that conversation, and knowing Cris, she would have heard it if she had been anywhere in the house. She was prudently sent away on a timely errand. After that turn of events, Cris determined she could never and would never become subject to the church. Not if such goings-on as that was allowed and condoned. She'd just have to take her chances of missing Heaven and going to Hell. At any rate, it couldn't be much worse than being forced to marry any old goat the 'dear sisters' decided to pick out for you to marry. And, if they were going to be in Heaven, maybe Hell would be preferable.

And so, she was out of the church. She was not only 'a backslider,' she refused, flatly, to attend the wedding. She couldn't bear the thought of having that big, burly, black lout for a father. She would have preferred anyone to him, even Mr. Benson. At least, if Mr. Benson was almost as plump and as old as Deacon Sayles, he was nice. Cris remained to live with Mom. Jeanie loyally supported Sooky. The girls were beginning to grow apart. Cris steadfastly refused to set foot in the Sayles house, and Jeanie, just as steadfastly, refused to be parted from Sooky. Mom tactfully but silently showed her disapproval of the impending wedding preparations by accepting and approving the move made by Cris.

Later, when they would all meet at church, Cris noted Sooky didn't look the part of a happy, radiant bride at all. She looked intimidated, bewildered, and sad. Deacon Sayles looked like a puffed-up pompous ass. He had a right to be elated. With the help of his cronies, and through some mumbo-jumbo, he exploited Sooky and the doctrine of the church in one swell swoop? He was entirely too ignorant to realize all the damage he and his cronies had done. They completely destroyed a child's faith and trust. Cris missed Sooky and Jeanie. She dearly loved Mom, but sometimes she wished she could have been more like Jeanie and been able to accept and adjust to the new events. Why couldn't she? She tried and promised to make herself go home with Jeanie and Sooky in spite of the 'Bear,' but when the time came for them to leave, she just couldn't do it.

Neither Mom nor Sooky tried to influence her either way. Wisely they didn't pressure her. They could sense the strain and the battle she was fighting. The 'Bear' didn't. He said her refusals and reluctance to accept him and all the generous things he would do for her was just pure impudence and insolence. He wanted to rule and boss all. He hated Cris because she wouldn't knuckle under him, and the feeling was mutual; Cris hated him too. She hated him mostly because Sooky was sad and dejected; even Jeanie was subdued. Cris knew something was wrong, but what she did not know.

"Mom?" asked Cris.

"Yeah, Cris," replied Mom.

Cris said, "Do you like him?"

Mom, taken by surprise by this question, stalled for time by asking, "Who? Like who? "Mom knew very well who Cris was talking about. She didn't know what she could or would say in answer and remain truthful without adding fuel to the fires of hatred already burning in Cris. "Well, I won't say or can't say I exactly like all his ways, but I do love his soul."

Cris said, "I hate him and his soul."

"Hush, 'Baby.' It ain't right for you to be thinking and talking like that. What yo' think Sooky'd say and how you think it make her feel if she was to hear you talking like that?" Mom replied.

"But, Mom...." said Cris.

"Hush, I said, Yo' mind what and where yo' talk," said Mom.

Cris replied, "What I was going to say was, I wouldn't say these things to Sooky. I don't want to hurt her more. It seems like she is hurt already."

Silence fell between them. Cris wandered aimlessly around the kitchen watching Mom finish the dinner preparations. It was almost time for dad to come home, and Cris wasn't satisfied yet with the answer she got. She had to know something else and didn't want to talk about it in front of him. But she had to know.

"Mom, what if Sooky has a baby?" Cris asked.

It had to come out in a rush. She hadn't planned to ask it that way, not quite so bluntly, but it was out. She knew Mom would not like her talking about things like that. But she had to know!

"What you know about people havin' babies? An' anyhow she married to him, and if she do, it's none of your affair. You tend to your own business and let grown people's alone."

Cris persisted, "That isn't what I mean. I mean, it would be my brother or sister. I just won't have it, that's all. Oh, I wish we had never even heard of that old church. I wish we had never gone there in the first place. I hate it, and I hate him!"

Mom opened her mouth to scold her for speaking that way, but a quick glance at her agitated face and the stark hatred in her blazing eyes struck Mom mute for the moment. Or was she silent because Cris had given voice to her own thoughts with her outburst? How could it be possible for this young child to contain so much hatred? How could she ferret out your secret thoughts and weaknesses as she could? She was uncanny. When Mom regained enough composure to speak evenly, she sent Cris to her room to study until time to set the table. Mom needed time alone to think. That conversation really shook her. Cris went, knowing full well she had struck 'pay dirt' and was entirely determined to press the matter further. There was a lot more she wanted to know, a hell of a lot more. However, she would bide her time to get the answers needed. And so she went, not to study, but to formulate questions and map her campaign with the skill of a seasoned general.

Even while she was planning her sortie, other more staggering events were in the making, these circumstances that would again change their lives. This time the change would be drastic.

Chapter 11

Only Sooky and Deacon Sayles were able to see all the pieces of the puzzle fall into place. Did what they saw cause them consternation? Did they try to juggle the pieces? Who knows? Cris noticed that Sooky looked sadder than ever, and Deacon Sayles was more churlish. She wondered if she could be a contributing factor or if she was the cause? No, it was something more than just her. She may have played a small part, but the real reasons went far deeper than that. Deacon Sayles was uncouth and demanding. His sexual drive was never sated. He knew he was past his prime years and, in his stupidity, thought to prove his masculinity through his prowess in the bedroom. He would not have known the word, much less its meaning, that described him in his ignorance. He was a sadist and knew nothing of the art of lovemaking or tenderness. All he knew or cared about was - she was female, and he was male. So, what more was there to know or care about? Sooky was completely asea. She had never been confronted with such a person before. She was no match for his possessive, selfish needs. She tried to submit dutifully, but the ungodly bestiality of his demands was destroying her. She would arise in the mornings, feeling bruised in body and soul. She felt defiled, her femininity abused and sexually degraded. Mom must have had an inkling of what was going on.

The two of them had almost daily telephone conversations. They were too close to be able to hide something as vital as this from one another. True, Sooky was a reticent person and always tried to solve her problems independently, but some part of this must have gotten through to Mom. Some part of it may have, but not nearly enough to cushion the impact of the crushing blow.

Sooky had to be hospitalized! It was a result of Sayles' violent outbursts. Oh, he was brutal and had shown his lack of control before, but he was like a crazed person this time. Like someone demented, and indeed he was. His jealousy, inadequateness, and ignorance took complete possession of his faculties. He had almost killed Sooky!

He had come upon Sooky and Jeanie one day as they were sorting and packing some boxes. They weren't expecting him home then, and they were intent on the task before them. They hadn't heard him come in, so his savage attack on Sooky took them completely by surprise. His first thought had been, "she's trying to sneak off and leave me." Without waiting or even asking for an explanation, he had struck. He swung Sooky's small body around and rained blow after blow on her frail frame. Her futile attempts to defend herself only served to enrage him more. Her strength was nothing to his. Had it not been for Jeanie, he would have killed her or done considerably more harm if that was possible. Dear loyal Jeanie did all she could against this maniacal onslaught. She hit him over the head with the stool Sooky had been so savagely snatched from. While the blow she delivered had no lasting effect, it did give them time to escape to the safety of the outdoors, where the neighbors could see them and hopefully help or shield them. Thank God for nosey neighbors; they can prove to be a blessing. This time they were a God-send. Sooky's recovery proved difficult, slow, and painful with many setbacks. She seemed old and worn without any of the fire and spirit she had always shown. It seemed she'd lost the will to fight or even live any longer. All her sparkle was gone. Sooky just wasn't Sooky anymore and was never able to make a complete physical or emotional recovery.

Mom had insisted Sooky come home with her on her hospital discharge. Sooky accepted without a murmur. She was far too weak physically and too drained and empty emotionally to protest. Anyway, she thought, "It will be nice to be pampered and be able to relax and rest. It will be so nice to know tenderness and love again." Sooky knew she had to have time to think. What was she to do? It was absolutely out of the question for her to even think of returning to Sayles. She could never even think of resuming her role as a wife to him. Sometimes she would drift into troubled, pain-racked sleep to awaken drenched in perspiration and shaking violently. Even in her sleep, she could not escape the nightmarish experience. Mom, God bless her, seemed never to leave her side during these terrible pain-filled hours. She was there soothing and comforting, trying to reassure and restore. Sooky was her heart, and now her heart was sorely wounded. She knew some of the wounds only God could heal.

Jeanie spent most of her waking hours with Sooky. She would sit with her by the hour and would reluctantly attend school. Jeanie would rush home to take up her vigil at Sooky's side. She seemed to fear a re-occurrence of the events leading up to this. It was necessary for her to see her, to be sure Sooky was alive and safe. This was a very traumatic experience for a young girl to witness. Her friends appreciated her feelings and respected her for them. They did continue to invite her to join them, but when she refused, they understood. They went their way without her and hoped she would feel free to join them soon. Only her boyfriend, Lee, refused to be put off. He would come and almost force her to get out and forget for a time. Jeanie and Lee fancied themselves in love, and

Lee was the faithful swain. He deserved to be thanked for helping Jeanie to regain her equilibrium.

Although Mom and Jeanie were dedicated to satisfying Sooky's needs as best they could, Cris would not go near her for some bizarre reason. She would not go in a room with her unless she was commanded and then would hastily complete whatever duty she had to perform and flee as if all hell's demons were on her heels. On the other hand, if Sooky felt well enough to be out of her room, Cris would be happy to take her needlework and sewing and sometimes pester or amuse Sooky. At any rate, she always provided some diversion for her. Cris could not feel comfortable in Sooky's room. There was something about that room she knew or felt but could not explain. Cris was a strange child with many unexplainable hunches; and thought it would be nice to have Jeanie and Sooky at home with her again. But there was too much of a chance to go back to the old pattern. In some way and for some reason Jeanie and Cris were no longer close. Cris felt alone, in a sense.

Mom and Jeanie were wrapped up in Sooky's care. Mom also had Dad, and Jeanie had Lee. What did she have? Nothing. For a time, she replaced Sooky in Mom's life, but now, she was in the background, practically forgotten. As soon as she could finish her chores and escape, she would take off for one of her favorite spots for reading. In nice weather, this was a spot high in the branches of a cherry tree and well hidden from ground view. Her presence was only apparent by the number of cherry pits dropped on unsuspecting heads. In inclement weather, her spot was in her room behind the large trunk placed in one comer of the room.

Cris had always been fond of reading and was in the habit of retreating to her favorite nooks where she could be alone to read and analyze what she had read. Only now, when she escaped, tentatively to read, she found her interest straying from the printed words on the pages she was absently turning. There were too many and much more important matters to be settled. These words printed in the books would be there for her whenever she wished, but these other matters needed attention now. They weighed heavily on her mind. For instance, all of the questions she had so carefully planned to ask Mom about were now of no importance. She wanted answers to the 'now' problems and causative to the 'now' problems. She needed something or someone to shed some light on them, so Cris listened carefully to all snatches of conversation she could manage to overhear between the adults. Guilty of eavesdropping, she was trying desperately to piece the story together. She turned to the Bible but instinctively knew some of the answers already but refused to believe them.

They appeared entirely too sinister for intelligent acceptance. Sisters Wishman and James had claimed their visions, dreams, and messages had come from the Lord, that the union between Sooky and Sayles was the will of the Lord from Heaven. If that were true, then why did it all have to end so hellishly? Simple. There were no God-given dreams, visions, or messages given to them. They lied. The reason was quite apparent. They merely wished to ensure a good and reliable source of income for the Church project they were officers of. Cris also suspected money was the chief reason Sayles was elected to the Deacon Board. As far as she could see, he certainly had no other attribute worthy of placing him there. Her answers were the only possible ones. She also knew Mom and Sooky would not be pleased to know she had these answers. They would say she was too young to understand things like that. True, she was young, but she understood a lot more than anyone gave her credit. Cris knew perfectly well that Sooky must have allowed herself to believed what they said. That wasn't too hard to understand.

Sooky had been raised to obey and to respect her elders; that older people wouldn't lead you astray. That was baloney. They were the ones who could and would because they had been there and knew all the ropes. Another reason was that Sooky had probably thought she was doing something good for the girls in her unselfish naivete. Cris fully realized Sooky was a young woman, attractive and desirable. A person who should love and be loved in return. But the thing she couldn't understand was how Sooky had ever been deceived, induced, persuaded, or forced to think, much less believe. Was Sayles the person for her? She wanted to ask Sooky, but she knew Mom would skin her alive if she were caught bothering Sooky with such questions. Then too, she had no idea of how Sooky would react about her asking such grown-up questions. Making up her mind, Cris felt nothing ventured, nothing gained. She would bide her time and catch Sooky alone and ask her. Every time she thought they might be able to talk, Sooky would have unexpected guests.

The only time she was alone was in her room and was either sleeping or resting. And Cris dreaded and feared that room, not Sooky. She supposed she loved her in her strange way. The fear and dread were due to the other 'presence' she was conscious of. Intuitively, she knew Sooky sensed 'It' lurking there, and she was afraid of it too. 'It' had to wait until 'It' was acknowledged before 'It' could claim Sooky. But Mom and Jeanie's love for Sooky and faith in God would keep 'It' cornered and at bay. Cris was quite vulnerable. But her faith was not as strong as she knew it had to be for her not to acknowledge 'It.' Nevertheless, she figured if that was going to be the only time and place Sooky would be alone, she would have to go in. Her love would have to be strong enough to keep 'It' at bay. It was destined for her to get answers to more than she ever dreamed of asking.

Cris was on the floor behind the trunk, reading, hidden from sight. She knew Jeanie was downstairs with Lee, and Mom was looking for her. Mom looked in their room and, seeing no one, had turned off the lights, muttering, "wonder where that Cris is?" "Jeanie, Cris down there?" "No, I think she went next door." "Well, you call her home about 9 o'clock." Cris had gone next door, but she had returned. It surprised her to hear Mom say she could stay out, even next door, until that late. Then it dawned on her that she wouldn't get her chance to talk to Sooky. But they wanted to talk and to know her whereabouts. That meant only one thing. They wanted to talk about something, and they wanted to be sure she wasn't around to overhear. Cris couldn't move from her place of concealment for fear of discovery, but from where she was, she was afraid she wasn't going to hear all that was going to be said. Oh, well, she would have to make the best of her lot. She didn't hear all, but she did hear enough to put two and two together. It set her mind to clicking. Boy, things were really popping. Before she could digest and file away one thing, something else was beginning.

She sure wished Jeanie wasn't so wrapped up in Lee. She could certainly use her help now. They were talking about a letter. Oh yes, that letter that came so long ago, the one telling them of a man's death. She remembered they argued whether or not they, the girls, should be told. No, no, wait a minute. They hadn't said whether the girls should be told; they said whether Jeanie should be told. It was all coming back to her.

Sooky said, "Jeanie should be told. He was her father, after all".

Mom replied, "T'won't do no good. She won't remember him. Yo' kids broke up and divorced long before she big enough to remember him." But they hadn't mentioned her! Not once did they say anything about her at that time.

She was so busy recalling those memories; she must have missed part of what was said and thought they were talking about her. No, it wasn't her they were talking about. It was another Cris, Her father! He was alive! Maybe they would say where he was. Did she miss that part? Her emotions ran riot. What right did they have to let her believe all these years that he was dead?

In her agitated emotional state, she disregarded that fact. The only reason she thought about it at all was that she had been eavesdropping. If she had been truthful with herself, she would have admitted it was not planned. It was all unintentional, and she wasn't supposed to hear it. She hadn't known when she climbed into her spot to read that they would be discussing something confidential. All she did was fail to let Mom know she was there. Like the other time so long ago, it wasn't her fault she could not fall asleep. Cris listened for more news, but the voices were lowered to a soft murmur. Well, she thought, 'that's all for tonight.' She climbed out over the trunk and crept stealthily down the stairs. Once downstairs, she was home safe. If Jeanie or Lee saw her, they wouldn't know if she was coming in or out. How could they know about her? They didn't know if they were going or coming. All they knew was that they were gloriously in love.

Cris kept this new information to herself as she had kept the other. She filed it away for further thought. Now was not the time to be inquisitive. To get anything more, she would have to take them off guard. Maybe, even play one against the other. Besides, if she brought it up too soon, she would have to admit she had been eavesdropping and that information, in the wrong hands, Mom's, for instance, could be hazardous to her backside if not to her health. She had enough facts tucked safely away to sort out at leisure and filed them away in her head to feel confident, someday, maybe soon, that she would have it all. Cris was precocious. That word, she overheard. Sooky used it in describing her. It had a nice sound to it, a pleasing sound to Cris. She made a mental note to look it up in the dictionary to find its meaning. The description matched her; she mentally matured at an early age.

After her overheard conversation, Cris was lucky enough to find Sooky alone, awake, and out of her room. Cris was elated. It should be safe to broach the subject now. She greeted Sooky affably and hurried into the house to change her school clothes and place her books in her room. Jeanie would be home soon, or else Mom would be standing guard. She wasn't quick enough and heard Mom return to the porch where Sooky was resting. Oh, well, maybe it was too soon anyway. She hadn't the time to think of how to bring up the subject intelligently and still not let Sooky know she had overheard them talking. Sooky's health was rapidly failing. She stayed in her room and in bed most of the time now. Mom wore a harried, worried look, although she put on a cheerful front whenever she was around Sooky. Poor Dad, he was completely pushed aside and ignored. Oh, Mom still cooked as well as ever and kept the house scrupulously clean, but her heart wasn't in it. Dad finally got tired of playing second fiddle and left. His leaving might have affected Mom, but at the time she was too engrossed in making broth and cooking other delicacies to try to tempt

Sooky's waning appetite to let it bother her. It was later that the full impact of his leaving hit her. It was too late then for an apology.

Jeanie's infectious laughter was a rare sound these days. She spent every moment she could with Sooky and seemed reluctant to leave her side. It was as if she thought by her very presence she could force strength and health into Sooky's frail body. Thank God for Lee. He was the only person who was able to coax Jeanie out and away from the house. He seemed to know Jeanie would soon need a shoulder to lean on, and he certainly intended to provide that shoulder. Cris refused to acknowledge any changes in Sooky's condition. She knew 'It' was lurking there in the shadows just waiting for acknowledgment, and she would show 'It' that she would never give in. She hoped that by showing her apparent unconcern, Mom and Jeanie would come to realize they, too, must deny 'Its' presence. They had to deny or else 'It' would take 'Its' tribute. She knew she was fighting a losing battle but was determined to hold out at least until the truth was revealed. Cris was a precocious child.

This particular afternoon, Jeanie was sent to town to do some shopping. Mom was busy in the kitchen concocting something to coax Sooky to eat. Cris was home because she hadn't wanted to accompany Jeanie. Jeanie wasn't fun to be with anymore. She wouldn't detour around to see the houses where all the painted women sat in the windows. Cris enjoyed looking at them. They were always dressed so fine, and their make-up made even the 'plain Janes' look good. Mom would have a 'cat-fit' if she so much as thought they were in that part of town. That fact, of course, only added spice to the sights for Cris. She figured what Mom didn't know wouldn't hurt her. Sooky was getting worse; Jeanie refused to gallivant around all over town with her to gawk at the ladies of the night. So Cris let her go alone. Her chores were finished, and there was no extra schoolwork she wished to do. She moped around, trying to find something to do, like sit with Sooky, but not in her room. Maybe she would persuade her to come downstairs.

Sooky was propped up in bed reading her Bible; Cris felt more than a twinge of concern as she looked at her. Sooky looked so small, frail, and childlike. Although the bed was only a three-quarter bed, it seemed to swallow her up. Cris, involuntarily, cast a furtive glance to the corner of the room. She was looking for 'It.' There was nothing visible, but she knew 'It' was there hiding in the shadows. There were crisp pink and white dotted ruffled curtains at the window and around her dressing table. The top of the table was uncluttered, holding only the necessary toilet articles and a few bottles of her favorite perfumes. The glass top was spotless. The nightstand held her reading lamp, pitcher, and water glass; the bottom shelf, for her books. A small extra table placed near her bed held the usual array of the bottles of ineffectual medicines. Sooky's Bible was usually found on her bed, within easy reach.

If Sooky was surprised to see Cris come in, she made no outward show. She smiled at the intruder and closed her well-marked Bible. Cris leaned over the bed to kiss her lightly on the forehead, thinking as she did, 'Gee, I'm still growing, and already I'm so much bigger than Sooky. I'll bet I could even pick her up if I wanted to.' Sooky was thinking, 'This is a surprise. Guess maybe she's growing up and getting over her funny ways. I certainly wasn't expecting her to come in and much less the kiss.' Sooky was frankly pleased by this impulsive show of affection from the undemonstrative Cris. To hide her embarrassment, Cris burst into a brief flurry of conversation, which soon dwindled into silence. She sat starring out of the window, resting her elbows on her knees and her index fingers pressing into her thin cheeks. This was a characteristic pose for her. She envied Jeanie's dimples and thought maybe she could force some indentations into her face by frequently pressing her fingers against them.

Sooky returned to her reading, seeming content and happy to have Cris there. After several occasional glances, which went unnoticed by Cris, Sooky broke the silence by asking, "What are you thinking about so seriously?"

"Why I don't have dimples like Jeanie," Cris replied.

"Well, I don't have any either," said Sooky.

Cris asked, "Then where did Jeanie get hers? From her father?"

I guess so. I never thought about it before, but I think he did have dimples," said Sooky.

Cris firmly replied, "Her dad's been dead for a long time now, but my Dad isn't. I sure wish I knew who and where he is now." This was said calmly and matter-of-factly as she turned to face Sooky. Cris wanted to leave no room for doubt. She didn't want Sooky to think she was only guessing. If Sooky could see her face, she would know she knew. Sooky saw and knew. Cris was sure her face or her words would not betray how little she actually knew and that she was fishing for more information.

Their eyes locked; Sooky's eyes fell, knowing the accusing insolent gaze of Cris. She unconsciously smoothed the coverlet on her bed with one hand while clutching her Bible tightly in the other. Cris's eyes opened wide in comprehension. She knew at that moment why nothing was ever said openly about her father. She was an illegitimate 'Love Child!" The shock and dismay that registered on Sooky's face told her that much. No, there was no need for words. She turned and rushed headlong from the room, almost colliding with Mom in the process.

Poor Mom. She misinterpreted the look on Cris's face to mean something was amiss with Sooky, and indeed there was, but it wasn't what she was expecting. Mom's heart raced in keeping with her flying feet as she rushed to Sooky's side. Thank God, Sooky looked the same physically, but Mom had never seen her so agitated and unsettled. What had that child been up to? What had she done before rushing out of Sooky's room with that strange expression on her face? What could possibly have happened to upset Sooky so and Cris enough for her to go slamming into her room? She hastily arranged the tray she was carrying and stood peering closely at Sooky and was shaking! Mom could see she was in no condition to explain anything now, so she would have to ask Cris what happened.

She crossed the hall and opened the recently slammed door. Cris was sitting on the side of her bed, staring intently at her feet as if she had never seen them before. She lifted her eyes briefly at Mom's intrusion and resumed her study. Mom was utterly baffled.

Mom asked, "What in the world had happened?" "Cris, what you do to Sooky?"

"Nothing," replied Cris.

"You had to do something to upset her like she is. I ain't going to ask you again. Now, what did you do?" Mom said.

"I told you, nothing. We were just talking, that's all." Cris said.

"Jes talking? Jes' talking don't upset nobody like that. An' why yo' sitting there looking like yo' jes' now found out yo' got feet? What yo 'do? What was yo 'talking about? Yo' bettah tell me I done tol' yo' and I ain't gonna ask yo' no mo,'" replied Mom.

Cris knew this was no empty threat. She thought she better say something, anything. "We were just talking about my father and where he is." She prudently did not add and who he is.

Mom asked, "Talking 'bout yo'? What you know? Who told?" Mom was so taken aback by what Cris said; she was rendered unable to finish one question before she would start another.

"I know everything. I know he's not the man who died. That was Jeanie's dad. I know he lives somewhere near, and I know why you don' talk about him." Cris replied.

Mom was dumbfounded. Had Sooky told Cris? How much did Cris really know? One could never tell with Cris. Just what had been said? Why had Sooky told her? The questions were spinning in Mom's head. She knew Cris wasn't being completely truthful. She knew she was holding something back; Cris's next words confirmed her worst fears.

"I know I'm illegitimate, I know I'm a bas... Cris never got a chance to finish the word. For all of Mom's bulk, she could move with lightning speed. Her hand shot out and connected with the side of her face. Cris was not quick enough to move out of the line of fire. Mom's voice was low and husky with rage as she asked, "You didn't say that to yo' Mother, did you? Yo' bettah had not. And I don't never want to hear you say that again to anyone. You hear me? Yo' just wait 'til I tend to Sooky an' I'll teach yo' to be so uppity to be talking like that. Where yo' hear such words, anyhow?"

Cris knew she had really put her foot in it this time, and an open confession might be good for the soul, but it sure could be hell for the behind. Ah, the price one must pay for knowledge. Since she knew she was in for it anyway, she may as well try to pry further. "Where is he?" Cris asked. Mom, in her anger, blurted the answer, "Spokane." As soon as it was out, she realized what she had been tricked into doing. She clapped a hand over her mouth, but it was too late now. It was out, and Cris was sitting there looking at her like the complacent imp she was. She turned sharply on her heels and went to comfort a now sobbing Sooky.

The big question had been answered. Cris was triumphant, and her scheme worked. She figured that if she could get them riled enough, one of them would slip. Chris decided against confiding in Jeanie because she wouldn't believe her anyway. Jeanie would have thought that she was only making it up. She would never believe anything like that about Sooky, or have the nerve to confront either of them with that kind of news and demand an answer. No, Jeanie wouldn't understand. To her, things that happened were passed, done, finished, and over. What was important to her were things here and now and maybe what was to be. Cris often wondered what she would think about this if she knew. This would really sit her back on her heels.

Jeanie had returned unnoticed in time to hear the last of Mom's words. She stood there looking questionably from Mom to a softly chuckling Cris. After Mom left, she asked, "What did you do? What did Mom mean? What are you laughing about?"

Cris laughed aloud, "I told her my idol had feet of clay."

"What do you mean? You're always talking in riddles, but it won't be so funny when Mom gets through with you." Jeanie flounced out, yet with a puzzled expression and her curiosity unsatisfied. She crossed the hall to Sooky's room, but she stopped and knocked discreetly on hearing the low murmur of voices. Mom opened the door a crack to tell her they were busy. Although the door had only been slightly ajar, it was wide enough for Jeanie to see Sooky was crying, and Mom was extremely upset. Now she was puzzled. What could Cris have done to cause all this commotion?

She stormed back to their room and was furious with Cris for having done something to hurt Sooky. She'd make Cris tell her what it was all about. She was the oldest and would force Cris to tell what happened. She looked at Cris, still sitting there with a half-smile on her face and rubbing her stinging cheek. She knew she might be able to get Cris to talk and tell her. Still, she knew, equally as well, if it were something Cris didn't want to talk about, Cris would and could elaborate and embroider whatever it was until she would be unable to make heads or tails of whatever it was anyway. Oh, Cris wouldn't deliberately lie but would merely veil the truth in riddles and mystery. Cris was a master at that. No, she decided, she wouldn't get any answers from Cris. Only if Jeanie could have heard what was being said behind Sooky's closed door.

When Mom had rushed in to comfort Sooky, she was met by wet, accusing eyes. Sooky said, "You told her." "I tol' her what? I ain't tol noboty nothin'. What all happen?" Mom asked.

Sooky looked closely at Mom. Her face showed only deep, pure and honest concern. Mom couldn't fake that look, but how and where had Cris gotten her information? Mom wiped Sooky's face soothingly with a damp cold cloth while Sooky haltingly told her what had gone on. "Cris came in and somehow started talking about Jeanie's dimples," said Sooky.

"What her dimples got to do with yo' saying I tol' her something?" Mom replied.

Sooky said, "Well, that's it. She was talking about Jeanie one minute and then switched over to talking about her father."

Mom asked, "Her father?" Mom's jaw dropped. "What she know 'bout her father?"

"That's just it, Mom. She knows, and I thought you had told her." Sooky said.

"I knows she knows, but I thought you had tol' her. She jes' tol' me that much." "That I tol' her?" "No, not that yo' tol' her, 'xactly, but that she knows 'bout," Mom's voice trailed off. She refused to say it. She refused to repeat Cris's words. Instead, she finished lamely, "That chile gets to be more of a problem every day."

Sooky nodded silently in agreement. She was busy trying to reconstruct the bits and pieces of information Cris could have gleaned over the years to have come to the conclusion she reached. They had always been so careful. They never talked about such things in front of the children. That letter, telling them of the death of Jeanie's father, had been burned, and all correspondence from Cris's father. Mom must have said something. She must have told her something.

"Mom, are you sure you never said anything? You know how Cris asks questions all the time," asked Sooky.

"No, I ain't said nothin'. In fact wasn't no need to. Cris ain't never said or asked 'bout it 'till now." Mom replied.

"Well, one thing is certain, she's not asking too much now. She's telling what she already knows." Sooky said.

"Now ain't that the truth." Mom replied.

"Mom do you think we or I should explain it all to her? Explain it all better, I mean?" Sooky said.

"No, she know too much already. Jes' let 'sleepin' dogs lie'. Twon't do no good to get it all stirred up again." Mom stood, absently stroking Sooky's forehead for a time. Sooky seemed lost in thought.

"Sooky?" Mom said.

"Yes?" replied Sooky.

"Guess I did speak out of turn." Sooky turned inquiring eyes to Mom.

"She, that Cris, said somethin' that made me so mad I jes' wasn't thinking what I say when she asked me where he be. I'm sorry." Sooky didn't respond, and Mom continued. "It jes' slipped out without me even thinking, and I answered 'for I knew what I was doin." The information Cris was seeking may have slipped out inadvertently without thought on Mom's part, but it certainly had taken a lot of thought and planning on the part of Cris to get it. Now it was all becoming clear. She had not been told, nor ever asked Sooky the details of her birth, yet somehow she knew. Had she known simply by looking at Sooky? Absurd! Impossible! There had to be a reasonable reason. Some word or something, but try as she would, she could not recall a single clue.

She delved within herself and now seemed to be emerging as another person. A wiser person, a knowledgeable person. Was reincarnation possible after all? Cris knew and understood why she and Sooky never had the close camaraderie Sooky shared with Jeanie. Cris was a constant reminder of something, someone that Sooky wanted to forget. Cris was her transgression personified. Now she knew why Mom doted on her. Mom felt sorry for her. The vague, disquieting stirring she felt for Sooky was now known. It wasn't jealousy. It was hatred. She always pushed it aside as being silly and uncalled for in the past, but now she knew its origin. She wondered, can love and hatred live so close? Is the dividing line that thin? She loved Sooky, didn't she?

If anyone told Jeanie she was witnessing the transformation and rebirth of Cris, she would have pooh-poohed the idea. All she saw was a sad and melancholy figure sitting quietly on a bed, waiting for the punishment Mom was sure to deliver. She didn't have the remotest idea of being a witness to Cris's taking a giant step.

Cris continued to sit and stroke her cheek while she silently and sincerely vowed never to accept pity again. No pity from anyone. She'd show them! Pity was not her cup of tea, and she would never permit it to be. Cris vowed she would make her way in life while having a ball doing it. She determined to leave her mark on all who knew her and maybe some who didn't. She felt she was ready to go out and conquer the world.

Finally, she shrugged to the window with that one large symbolic step. Jeanie saw her shudder, but she imagined it was due to the thought of her impending punishment. Poor naive Jeanie. How little she knew her baby sister, but nobody really knew Cris. Nobody really knew the workings of her mind. All Jeanie knew was that Cris still looked the same to her and was just as annoying as ever. Even more so, if that were possible since Cris was not giving her any insight into the present events. (It would be many years later before Cris confided in Jeanie.)

While taking that one step to the window, a part of a Bible verse popped into her mind. "Wisdom is better than strength." Well, if wisdom was better than strength, she'd be the wisest person since King Solomon. She'd be the wisest of the wise if need be. Maybe she wouldn't make it academically, but she would be wise in the ways that would count. Cris now appeared to have set a pattern for each day, and she had a new goal to be reached. It was as if she knew exactly where and how far she must be every new day. Like she lived these days before as if life now was a repeat performance in some strange manner. It seemed as if she knew what to expect from life, but not exactly just when to expect it.

Cris didn't agree at all with the theory Mom and Sooky had adapted: 'Let sleeping dogs lie.' She wanted to learn more about the why's and to be certain of her facts. What was her father's attitude toward her? What was he like? Was she very much like him? These and so many other things she had to know. She got the information and filed it away. Her storehouse of wisdom was growing.

After that incident, things on the surface were back to normal. Mom and Jeanie continued their tender ministrations even though it was apparent that Sooky's health was steadily and rapidly worsening. Cris elected to ignore as much of the change as she could and became more withdrawn.

In the few months left, preceding Sooky's death, Cris matured rapidly. Her scarcely nubile breasts seemed to burgeon overnight. This caused Sooky and Mom to worry. They could rest easy, however. Nothing was wrong. Her body simply had to ripen to keep pace with the mental expansion she was experiencing. Cris had no time for indiscriminate sexual activities. For years, she knew that the stork didn't deliver babies, and neither were they found under cabbage leaves. What she didn't have knowledge of was the complete details of her origin.

Cris remembered how furious she had been the afternoon of the unjust scolding for walking home from school with one of the older boys. Sooky saw them pause at the stairs leading to their yard to chat for a brief moment. Ray had playfully thrown his arm around her shoulders and hugged her before jogging off to catch up with the other fellows. Since that was the extent of the encounter, Cris was dumbfounded, appalled, and then indignant at the severity of the scolding. Her indignation slowly gave way to unleashed the furious speech as Sooky's voice continued to assault her ears. Sooky's tirade ended with, "Ray is much too old and experienced for you to be going around with. Now, I don't mind you coming home with a group of youngsters, but not with just one boy. A girl has to be careful; you know." Cris boldly said, "Sure, I know... but... it's too bad you didn't know to be careful. But then, if you had practiced what you are now sputtering at me, I wouldn't be here to hear it, huh?" Cris didn't wait for an answer after her short surprising outburst. She stormed out of Sooky's room and into her own to throw herself headlong on the bed before giving way to the torrent of body-wracking sobs. She hadn't done anything wrong, so why was it insinuated she did? She knew she had hurt Sooky badly by her reply and felt she might have been unfair, but then why not? Hadn't Sooky hurt her and been quite unfair with her?

Her sobs gradually ceased, and she lay there thinking, "Boy, she must really have a guilty conscience. She can't trust anyone. What could she possibly find wrong with me just walking home with a boy, be he young or old and in broad daylight and public? Nothing. Absolutely nothing! Unless the relationship between Sooky and my father had also started as innocently. Could that be it?" She lay there wondering and conjecturing until she heard Mom call. That was their only real outspoken confrontation, but the hostility and bitterness were there just under the surface.

Cris would often find Sooky watching her with disturbed and troubled eyes. Cris would return the look with hard cold eyes, eyes filled with hatred and questions. It seemed whatever feeling or love she had been capable of feeling for Sooky was now doubled in hatred. In later years she often pondered the oh-so-very thin line dividing love and hate. She also learned that hate saps and destroys, so she replaced the hatred with a modicum of tolerance. Tolerance devoid of compassion, however. And learning compassion wasn't a show of weakness but a very desirable trait.

Chapter 12

Sooky's death prostrated Mom and Jeanie with grief, although it hardly caused a ripple of emotions in Cris. Oh, she was subdued and sad, but not entirely from grief for Sooky. She was mourning for herself and thinking she had lost the last chance of gleaning all the information she wanted to have. Mom and Jeanie regarded her with dismay. How could she possibly be so unfeeling? Some of Mom's contemporaries said she was reacting in shock. How very wrong they were. Cris was not reacting at all, and she was not unfeeling. She cut off any feeling she felt for Sooky. Her wish was to explain this to Mom, but she couldn't. Mom was blinded and deafened by the enormity of her loss and misunderstood Cris's explanation.

Mom interpreted it to mean that she didn't care at all. Cris didn't bother to talk to Jeanie about it; she would have never understood. She and Jeanie had grown too far apart to have much in common anymore. Jeanie and Lee married soon after Sooky's death, and that too, Cris appeared oblivious.

Cris enjoyed being the center of Mom's attention, and they grew to be quite close, that is, as close as Cris would permit anyone to be. The relationship was good for Mom. She felt so lost and empty now that Sooky was gone and Dad left. Ministering to Cris helped to restore her. (Chalk one up in favor of Cris.)

In all fairness to Cris, she did miss both Sooky and Jeanie, but not in the sense of beloved family members, but as friends no longer around. Oh, she saw Jeanie infrequently, but their separation was rapidly becoming more and more apparent. Jeanie had a new life and friends with the young marrieds, and Cris was definitely not a part of that life. Cris was also busy building a new life for herself, and Jeanie was certainly not a part of those plans, at least not at that time. Maybe Jeanie would be useful later but not now. Sure, it was fun to go to some of the places Jeanie would occasionally take her and doing things Mom would never have permitted her to do alone. Jeanie either, for that matter, if she knew of the places they sometimes went. Since Jeanie was married, she no longer had to get Mom's permission or 'kow-tow' to her or anybody else. That fact was filed away for future action. Right now, marriage was not a part of her plan. She wanted to finish school and try to meet her father.

School was fun and easy for Cris and didn't tax her brain. Therefore, she had plenty of time to learn much more than the usual academic lessons. She learned many things that would stand the tests of time and manipulate to get her way. She learned a reverence and strong determination would and could get almost anything she desired, but also that it would speed things up to find and use some shortcuts. That was where perseverance would be of the greatest use. It would make finding the shortcuts much easier. The first shortcut Cris tried ended at a dead-end. The Great Depression was really making itself felt and was putting the squeeze on everyone. Mom's work was evaporating, and the needs of Cris were enlarging. No one had the money to spend on luxuries, so the cleaning lady and the laundry woman were among the first to be cut out. The few available jobs were mostly live-in, and no one could afford or wanted to hire a woman with a young dependent, so Mom was out. As the few nice pieces of jewelry Mom managed to accumulate disappeared to help make ends meet, Cris thought, 'We are going backward. Things are as bad almost as when we were in the little brown house.' In truth, things were worse because they hadn't missed what they had never had. They became accustomed to better living conditions, and it proved a hard and bitter pill for Cris to swallow. She knew how much it pained and grieved Mom to have to give up her prized possessions.

An Evangelistic group was trying to found a commune-type dwelling. They asked Mom to join them as a cook. They told her frankly the pay would be poor, practically nil, but she and Cris would be part of the organization, so she would not have the expense of keeping up a household. They also pointed out that Cris would be able to earn a small amount and be helpful to them as a babysitter of the minor children of those parents fortunate enough to find employment. They would all share and benefit alike. Mom was skeptical of the group's success with this type of living, but it was a job. She figured if it didn't work out, they could always leave. They were a migrant group following various harvests and crops. She was worried about proper schooling for Cris, but they assured her that the youngsters would be able to enroll in the local school with no difficulty. Cris encouraged Mom to join. The novelty of the arrangements intrigued her, and she thought there was a possibility that the group might travel to where her dad might be.

Eventually, they did get to the right place, but poor Cris, who usually planned so carefully, really goofed. Mom flatly and stubbornly refused to divulge any more information about her father—no name other than Cris. No address, nothing. She would have to depend on pure luck this time, and 'Lady Luck' looked the other way.

Cris found herself in a strange town, among strangers whom she couldn't and wouldn't confide in or pry any information out of without making public her purpose. She knew Mom would be most unhappy with her if she did. Mom's unhappiness wasn't what deterred her. It was what that unhappiness would do to her backside that stopped the public disclosure. She tried in a very amateurish adolescent way and failed dismally. A less determined person would have been sorely discouraged and ready to give up, but not Cris. She only pulled back long enough to regroup her thoughts and efforts to make new plans. She came to the following conclusions:

1) The group elders kept a too watchful eye and heavy restraining hand on the youngsters. Cris figured if she could get a chance to be alone and be able to roam the town freely to look in the right places (wrong according to the Evangelistic Group), she might find him. She was sure she would know him and was equally sure he would know and welcome her if ever they would meet.

2) There wasn't one of them she was able to take into her confidence. The youngsters were entirely too 'namby-pamby' for her likes, like a bunch of scared rabbits.

3) Therefore, she and Mom would have to return home, and she would start from there again. Cris wouldn't have much trouble convincing Mom that life here wasn't for them. Mom did not like the nomadic existence; they would return home to pick up the pieces of a needlessly, futile interrupted life. Cris, for once, would study like hell to catch up with her old schoolmates. She would get caught up and continue in High School, chafing securely under the restrictions of proper conduct imposed by her Mom. There would be no movies, no makeup, no dancing, no nothing. To her, it was all the same as no life. It's not that she didn't

attend movies; she played hooky whenever she wanted to see a movie. She would be permitted to go with Jeanie, and they loved to dance, and Cris would be able to wear all the makeup, she pleased, even if she did wipe it off carefully before coming home. This would allow her to do most of the things she wanted to do, but it irked her to sneak to do them. There would have to be a way out.

BACK HOME

Her way out could come in the form of marriage. It seemed an epidemic of marriage was spreading. Kids, who barely tolerated each other, were suddenly, supposedly gloriously in love and getting married. Cris refused to be outdone and wanted to be married, but she didn't fool herself into believing that love would find her. She was going to use it as a way out.

This time she planned much more carefully, learning things first. She needed to win Mom over to her way of thinking, and that was going to be quite a battle. Mom felt the kids were much too young to be thinking of marriage. Furthermore, most of them hadn't even finished high school. Mom urged Cris to finish and go to college (like her mother would have wanted) but, Cris was determined to be among the first of the crowd to marry. It took a significant bit of cajoling and a few acts of conduct, which was not entirely up to Mom's approval, to prove to Mom, some things could be worse than marriage… so, Mom gave in shall we say?

Cris now set to work in earnest. None of the local lads she knew would make a suitable husband. Their families would be too close, and with Mom around too, it would be more than Cris could take. No, it would have to be a boy from out of town. But who? She didn't know many of them very well, but then, one would be as good as another for her purpose. She thought an excellent time to choose would be while she and Mom attended one of the annual Church confabs. It seemed like the right timing. Now, all that was necessary was to get one of the boys interested. That shouldn't prove too hard. She wasn't exactly unattractive, and she could be quite seductive if need be; the need was definitely there since the ratio was three to four (not in favor of the weaker sex).

She chose her wardrobe with as much oomph as she thought Mom would go for and what she desperately wanted. The competition was going to be rough. Most of the other girls were older than her and therefore had more freedom where the boys were concerned. Oh well, she would snag one, anyone, and one was all that was needed.

The event was only to last three days, and she already wasted a whole day picking, choosing, and discarding the boys. She knew she must hurry yet pick carefully. Whoever the lucky one was, had certain criteria he had to measure up to. He had to be someone Mom couldn't find too much fault with; also, he had to be someone she felt she could manipulate. This was important. She figured she could bring Mom around to her way of thinking. Cris waived her color requirement. There simply weren't enough 'color-right' prospects available. Oh, well, maybe she could turn that into a bonus advantage.

Once her choice was made, she zeroed in for the kill. The quick surrender of her prey should have served as a warning that something was amiss, but Cris was too engrossed in her scheme to take proper notice. If she paid attention to the happenings, she would have seen the relief mirrored on the faces of his parents when they noticed the undue attention their son was paying to Cris. They were relieved to know 'Sonny Boy' had found a young, innocent, pure girl. 'Sonny Boy' had been causing a few raised brows back home by his relations with a not too young widow. Mom tried not to worry too much about the turn of events and wanted to tell herself that it would not be serious, that it would be the usual boy-girl affair. But Cris had other plans and so did Sonny Boy.

She was in. The letters flew back and forth, thick and fast. Each seemed determined to outdo the other in attesting their undying, ever-lasting love and devotion.

Since some of her friends were planning early summer weddings, Cris naturally set her date for late spring. They could follow her if they wished, but she would be the first. She couldn't care less if everything was up to Amy Vanderbilt's standards. All she was interested in or cared about was being the first and making it as difficult as possible for the follow uppers to outdo her.

Notwithstanding, her wedding was beautiful. The Church seemed a bower of spring flowers; Cris was the typical blushing bride and Mom the usual tearful mother of the bride. Her wedding night was a nightmare. She was rushed into being a dutiful wife by a well-experienced mate. She hated her role and lost no time in letting her spouse know how she felt. Her reluctance only excited him more. Boy, had she, the tricker, been tricked! She grew to hate him, and if the truth were known, he probably hated her too. Cris was bound to make the best of a bad bargain. Marrying Sonny Boy was a means of escape, and now she was more trapped than ever.

SHE WAS PREGNANT!

Her shortcut proved to be a long, tedious detour with no immediate end in sight. Now, what was she to do? The fact that

Sonny Boy spread his charms as freely and as indiscriminately as thistledown in the wind was of no consequence to Cris. She felt the more outside activity he had, the less she would be bothered. Mom was appalled by this turn of events. She tried to talk to Sonny Boy after utterly failing to reach Cris. She tried to explain that Cris led a sheltered life without the benefit of having the guidance of a father. Cris had never been entirely told of the responsibilities of being a wife, that underneath, Cris was just a child playing at being grown. Sonny Boy tuned her out.

The marriage lasted long enough for Cris to become a mother and pregnant again before Sonny Boy took off to greener pastures.

For a time after the marriage had ended, Cris seemed at loose ends. She adored the children, although somewhat in awe of them. She treated them like live dolls and played, bathed, and dressed them much as a child would with a new and amusing toy. When she tired of them, she left them to Mom's tender keeping and care. Cris realized somewhere along the way she had gotten off track. Giving herself a mental shake, Cris started backtracking to find the wrong turn she took. Some things couldn't be changed, they would have to be accepted, and some needed to change. She prayed and hoped to have the sense to know which was which. Her goals, set long ago, had yet to be attained, but they would be. She promised herself to do it. Making her mark on the world and finding her father was what she must do.

Things weren't as bad as they appeared on the surface. She was her own boss at last, and she fully intended to enjoy that accomplishment. Cris had two lovely children, the only really good thing that came out of her brief marriage. Thanks to Sonny Boy, she knew a lot more about men. Now, all that was left was to become self-supporting.

Since she had no technical, practical work training, employment was hard to find. Somewhere in her search for work, the idea of making easy money while working at home was suggested. It appealed to her. She would be home with the children and yet have an income. They said the idea was to buy chickens and raise them to fryer size and sell—nothing to it. 'Just buy the chickens at the hatchery, feed 'em, and sell.' 'Keep them warm, dry, and clean.' They said.

No one told her how hard it was to keep them warm, dry, and clean. Keeping the chicks alive long enough to reach fryer size; was hard work. Cris found she could keep them dry and clean fairly easily, but the little chicks appeared determined to keep themselves warm, even if it meant smothering themselves to do it. Her first attempt was a fiasco. Over half of the chicks smothered. She had gone out early to feed them and clean the chicken house before taking the children to see them. When she opened the door and stepped inside, she let out a gasp of dismay. There they were! The little idiots! They had all crowded and piled into one corner of their area and smothered. Tears of frustration and fury stung her eyes as she discarded the dead chicks and separated those still alive. No need of crying, she told herself firmly. Do something. She was sure if she partitioned their area better and kept a fire going in the shed all night, the chicks wouldn't crowd together. She tried. Some of the colder nights found Cris, wrapped in blankets, spending the night in the chicken house, keeping the fire going.

Not only was it difficult to raise the chickens, but it was also hard to find a market for them. The larger poultry houses had most of the markets sewn up, and if she were to sell them to a commercial market, they had to be inspected and etc. Cris was reduced to house-to-house sales, and that meant more hard work.

The chickens had to be killed, picked, cleaned and peddled. Mom and Cris worked almost as hard as Mom and Sooky did so long ago, with no better financial results.

Your own boss, huh! Great! This was enjoying being your own boss?! This was progress?

Chapter 13

Cris often wished for the security of her early childhood, even the restrictions imposed on her by Mom. Now she knew and appreciated what it meant to be the breadwinner in the family. So, it was no great wonder she was easy prey to any get rich scheme which might come her way, and come they did.

One day, while delivering and taking orders for chickens, she ran into a former schoolmate, Beatrice. Only now, she called herself Bebe and was the madam of one of the houses Jeanie and Cris were forbidden to go near when they were children. Bebe didn't appear abashed at meeting Cris again in her new role, and really why should she have been? She was expensively dressed and coiffured, while Cris actually looked dowdy in comparison. Bebe invited Cris in for coffee and a cigarette to talk over old times. Cris didn't smoke and should have refused, but she wished to appear a 'woman of the world,' so she accepted and coughed uncontrollably, just trying to light the thing. Bebe laughed uproariously.

Cris was nervous and ill at ease, but since Bebe promised to become a very lucrative customer, she felt she couldn't offend her. Bebe told her the girls always seemed to like fried chicken, and they always seemed to be hungry. Furthermore, she laughingly added, "That's something tasty they can snack on between cus..., ah, their work."

Cris was all eyes and ears. Her mind was awhirl. She nodded and hoped she was giving the right answers at the right times, but her mind was far afield from whatever Bebe was saying. There were so many things she would have liked to ask her, and her question had nothing to do with how many fryers she wanted each week. Cris finished her coffee and rose to leave. "Thanks for the coffee, Beatrice, and thanks loads for the order. See ya' soon." She made the rest of her deliveries in a preoccupied state. After the last delivery of the day, she didn't even try to get any new customers. She wanted to go home and think, to sort out her thoughts. Bebe led a life of comparative ease here while she toiled long hours to make half as much money. How come? She knew or felt she had as much 'grey matter' if not more than Bebe. The seed was planted, maybe not during that first conversation or the ones which followed, but it was definitely planted.

Bebe, with or without design, made her life seem exciting and glamorous as well as easy; Cris would glance at Bebe's long polished nails and smooth hands, then back to her broken nails and work-roughened hands. It was unfair. She was fighting a battle with herself. All that Bebe stood for was against what she had been taught from childhood and through her life. But, she could feel herself weakening. The chicken business was improving, but, oh, so slowly. There were so many things she wanted. There were things she wanted to do and have for herself and the rest of her family. The children could use so many things that they had to do without because her budget just couldn't be stretched to cover them. And there was Mom. She always worked so hard; it was time things were made easier for her. And the main thing was that she hoped to be able to continue her search for her father. She knew that would take money, and right now, all they were doing was barely breaking even. The seed had taken root.

Maybe, just maybe, mind you, if she worked for Bebe for a short time, she could get some money saved up. After all, she reasoned, she had been married and knew something about men. No, she couldn't do it. The idea was too preposterous to even think about. What would she tell Mom? She'd have to have some plausible excuse for being away from home.

There was no reasonable thing she could think of which would sound even halfway appropriate for the hours she would be away to work for Bebe. No, that was out of the question. She would have to think of some other way to increase their income. But, the seed was growing.

Cris and Mom discussed means of improving their lot. Mom knew how hard it was for the women to raise a family and provide for them. She knew the many pitfalls and temptations a young woman could fall prey to and also sensed Cris had been wrestling with a problem lately. She agreed with Cris to sell out the chickens and moving to the nearby larger city where chances for employment were much better.

Something seemed to be brewing. Many factories and plants were stepping up production and hiring. More families were, therefore, able to hire more help, and the pay was getting better. A lot of the papers were carrying ads for Apartment house managers and caretakers. They surmised if they could find a job like that, it would be much easier for them. They would have a rent-free apartment plus have a steady monthly income.

Cris applied at many places, but the answer was always the same. "Sorry, what we had in mind was a couple. We need a man for the heavier work. You know, repairing and such." Cris was disappointed again and again. In desperation, she took a job doing day work. She was thoroughly disgusted and wasn't progressing. Things went from bad to worse. More and more frequently, she toyed with the idea Bebe had given her. Why couldn't she work for a time? Just long enough to get a few dollars ahead? What could be the harm in that if it bettered their standard of living? She wouldn't have to tell Mom the full details. All she would and did say was that she would spend a weekend with one of her former schoolmates. Since Bebe's place was out of town, who was going to be the wiser? No one, she figured. How very wrong she turned out to be.

Her first weekend netted barely a few dollars over what she had earned on her domestic job. It appeared part of what she made would go toward obtaining suitable working clothes for her. Also, part of her earnings found their way into the madam's kitty. She was ready to throw in the towel in more ways than one and call it a day. However, the other girls urged her to stick with it and give it a fair shake. They said she would have steady customers of her own, and also, there were rumors that a lot of servicemen would soon be in the area, which they said always meant good times. She decided to continue for a time and see, although her intuition told her to quit. Now!!!

True to their word, the next weekend, the place was jumping. Everyone was busy. For a time, Cris was able to keep track of her earnings. Boy, in just a few hours, she had made more than she had made all week scrubbing floors and washing down walls. This was going to get her ahead faster than she ever dreamed possible. Her mind was reeling with all the possibilities she envisioned opening up for her. All feelings of guilt were drowned in the clink of silver and the rustle of paper. She had struck up a friendship of sorts with one of the girls, Kelly, an 'ofay' chick. On this night, she and Kelly had planned to go uptown for dinner as soon as Kelly's old man came by. Cris hoped he would bring his friend, Doug, with him. Maybe they did come by, and they, the girls, were busy. Maybe they were late getting there. Maybe they should have gone to dinner without waiting for them. The main thing was, they stayed on and worked.

Cris was pleased with the way she looked tonight. Her hair was done page-boy style, and it fell around her shoulders in a thick, soft mantle. She preferred a simple hair-do when working. It was easier to comb and keep in place. Tonight, she was wearing a floor-length pleated silk jersey with a tightly fitted bodice and midriff. She was proud of her small waistline and spared no pains to show it off. Not bad, kid, she thought as she paused in front of the mirror at the top of the stairs, Not bad at all.

The mirror reflected a tall, well proportioned young woman in a softly clinging cerise dress, whose face was carefully, though overly made up. There was a provocative flash of silver sandals beneath the swirl of her pleats. Cris surveyed her image with critical eyes. Her eyes were large, bright, and sparkling with excitement. By the time she reached the foot of the stairs, these same eyes would be dark, mysterious, alluring, and quite inviting.

Cris was about to enter the overcrowded parlor when Maggie, the maid, almost bowled her over to notify the girls that the place was being raided before she disappeared out a little-used door that opened into a narrow walkway that led to the street. Cris was hot on her heels, but her long skirt hampered her speed. As she burst through the door, it was not to dash to freedom but into the arms of the biggest policeman on the force. "Not so fast, Sister. You ain't planning on going without your friends, are ya?" He backed her into the hall where the other girls stood huddled in various states of dress or, in most cases, undress.

After that, things happened so fast poor Cris couldn't keep up. She didn't know what she was supposed to keep up with anyway. She was caught up in a whirlwind of activity, and when the wind died down, she found herself being fingerprinted and mugged. "Well," she thought ruefully, At least I look my best." That thought brought her little comfort. She thought no one would know? Ha, that was a laugh. Anyone who could read would know, now. Good Lord! Mom! The children! How was she ever to face them?

Cris felt doomsday had come when she heard the heavy clank of the massive steel doors behind her. She collapsed on her hard bunk in tears. The other girls chatted, laughed, and cursed the 'City's finest' for not giving Bebe their usual warning. Someone spoke up, "Ya know, maybe she did know and figured since this was payday, she'd take a chance."

"Could be. She's so damned money-hungry."

"Yeah," another voice chimed in, "You don't see her down here with us, do you?"

"She must have known," this from Kelly, "That bitch never leaves the joint when there is money around unless she..." Her voice was drowned in a growing mutter of threats and dire promises of what each would do to Bebe when they met. Cris and her tears were ignored. This incarceration was an 'old hat' to them. They knew these things happened periodically, but usually, they had warnings. They would take turns in being caught. This time was the first time they had all been picked up at the same time. Bebe must not have made her pay-off.

Jeanie came to her rescue, bailed her out, and took her home. Oh, yes, Jeanie bailed her out and took her home, but not without letting Cris know just how magnificent, forgiving, and understanding she was being. Cris was grateful to Jeanie for giving her freedom again, but she was sickened by Jeanie's holier-than-thou attitude. She knew full well Jeanie hadn't exactly lived a saintly life. She had just been luckier and had not gotten caught as soon as she.

Mom was heartbroken but forgiving. She felt she had failed with Cris. Her only recriminations were directed against herself. That was harder for Cris to take than all of Jeanie's berating.

Marian Hunter & Gloria King

Chapter 14

By now, war was declared, and jobs were popping up all over. Cris was working hard, honestly and honorably, in one of the factories. She was doing O.K., but she was still not satisfied and hadn't given up looking for her father. She decided to quit her job and go to where he was last known to be. Cris was reasonably sure that getting a job there would be no problem, hoping her pursuit of her father would bear fruit. This was a good excuse to go. The truth was, she was ashamed to stay and face Mom and the children after her disastrous episode.

She secured a small apartment, a good job, and the most intense feeling of loneliness she had ever known. Cris was a good worker, and the job proved interesting as well as lucrative for her. She made advancements rapidly. Her guilty feelings caused her to go home on weekends laden with gifts for Mom and the children. The time at home would be filled with happy chatter and descriptive stories of her work and co-workers. Monday would find her back on the job, as lonesome as Friday had found her. She knitted, crocheted, read, sketched, and spent hours cleaning her small apartment until it fairly sparkled, and she was still lonesome. Some evenings she would go for long walks, alert for a glimpse of a familiar face.

She took to dropping into the neighborhood tavern for a beer or two and a bit of conversation before turning in. One evening, while sitting there sipping a beer and exchanging banter with some of the regulars, the stares of an older man seated alone in one of the booths caught her attention. Her casual glance told her nothing except he was studying her face intently and with a puzzled expression on his face. She wondered what his story was and seemed harmless. He left soon after that without even speaking. Through idle curiosity, she asked the bartender who he was when he came by to refill her mug.

"Ted, who was that? The little guy who just left?" Ted laughed, showing amazingly even white teeth in a quite handsome face, "Funny you should ask about him. He's been asking about you. That's Howie Johnson. What you guys doin'? Carrying on some kind of long-distance romance?"

"No, nothing like that...yet. I just wondered that's all." Then added, "It's kind of creepy the way he was staring." Ted leaned across the bar to pat her hand in a playful, greatly exaggerated gesture of reassurance while saying with mock seriousness, "Don't you worry about him. Old Ted'll take care of your fine brown frame." Cris entered the spirit of the exchange and flipped back with, "Who says I'm worried? Could be I'm interested. Could be I..." Whatever else she was going to say was cut short by a commotion outside the door. In her inimitable way, Dolly was about to make another of her dramatic entrances, or, in this case, re-entrance. Mike had taken her home just a few minutes ago, but Dolly, like McArther, would and did return. Cris was flabbergasted. In the short time she had been gone, Dolly had managed to fall, braise her knee, tear her stockings, lose her purse, and in general give the appearance of having been drag through a knot-hole.

Now she lurched through the door and made her unsteady way to a booth, muttering all the while, "No son of a bitch gon' tell me when to go home or what to do, I'll do as I damned well please," and then raising her voice, "Bring me a double Muscatel." She had expended herself and crumpled into a sobbing dejected heap in the corner of the booth. Her hair was hanging in straggling wisps about her face. She raised a dirt begrimed hand to push it back, leaving an uneven streak across her forehead. Kate and a couple of the other girls went to her rescue. Between supporting her on each side and someone holding up the rear, they managed to get her out and home. Mike would take over from there and put her to bed.

Dolly was a grand person when she was sober. It was a source of amazement to Cris, and most people who knew her knew that anyone could reach the state of intoxication after a couple of drinks. Mike knew and understood Dolly as few people did. She was intelligent, free-hearted, and basically good. (All the harm she did, she did to herself.) From bits of gossip and snatches of conversation, Cris pieced the story together. Dolly had been married but was still in love with her former husband and turned to drinking as a means of forgetting her troubles and frustrations. Dolly had been quite good-looking at one time, but her many bouts with the bottle were erasing all vestiges of beauty. Her face was scarred due to drunken falls, or, as Cris was inclined to believe, some drunken brawl with one of the men who gave her shelter from time to time. She had a few teeth missing, and when she was sober, she was careful not to smile too broadly.

It was true, Dolly would work, but it was equally true she was unable to hang onto her money long enough to take care of herself properly. Mike tried keeping a part of her earnings to put up against lean times when she could not work. He tried keeping liquor at home for her. And anything and everything he could think of to help her, but when Dolly wanted her money, she wanted it then and there. The liquor he provided at home only served to whet her appetite for more. Mike honestly was no match for Dolly's colorful verbal tirades, nor would he resort to physical abuse to stop her.

Mike relegated to waiting for Dolly to stagger home on her own or, as more usually the case, be brought home for his tender ministrations. Kate and Cris tried befriending Dolly, figuring some of her problems stemmed from loneliness. They, as well as Dolly, refused to admit she was a typical alcoholic. They would ask her to go shopping with them, over to sew, or just chat. Their invitations were always gladly accepted, although, on many occasions, Dolly was unable to carry out her part of the bargain. It seemed no one or nothing was going to come between Dolly and the bottle.

Seeing the disastrous effects of the 'Battle of the Bottle,' Cris changed her routine of daily stops at the tavern. God knows she didn't want to become a second Dolly. She could see and understand how easily it could happen. Nothing was exciting or titillating about going to work, grocery shopping, and returning home to an empty house. It could and did get damned lonesome and depressing.

She was no nearer the end of her search than when she had first come. Cris missed Mom and the kids more than she wanted to admit. In a word, she was about ready to admit defeat and go home when something happened to change her mind. Cris had returned to her sweltering apartment from a shopping spree. The weather was hot and muggy, and she felt sticky and uncomfortable. She tumbled most of her packages helter-skelter on the bed and kicked off her shoes before taking her groceries into the kitchen. 'Whee, it sure gets hot here. I was a nut to go traipsing all over town. I must be going off my rocker. No one with good sense would work all day and then tramp all over town afterward, not as hot as today. 'But if I'd really looked, I could have found all I wanted at Wards and lots cheaper too,' she thought as she opened doors and windows to get the benefit of any stray breeze. Her head was throbbing, her stomach rumbling, and her feet were burning. She put a pot of coffee on the stove and a casserole in the oven before running a tub of cool water. She was bushed, roasted, famished, but pleased with herself, nevertheless. Not only had she bought things for Mom and the children, but she also splurged on herself—sandals, hose, bag, and dress.

She rummaged through the things on the bed to find the dress box and ripped it open excitedly. She shook the dress out and held it in front of her as she twirled before the mirror. The sound of coffee perking over on the stove cut her preening short. She drank her coffee while trying to decide whether or not to wear her dress at home, when she went out or save it for the Elk's dance which was coming up soon. She looked at the clutter of bundles on the bed. 'Boy, I'm really gonna have to be on short rations till next payday.'

She was practically broke but happy. She hummed contentedly through her bath and dinner. Her kitchen cleaned, she moved her packages and luggage into the front room where it was cooler and set about packing for her trip home when a knock at the open door interrupted her. 'Bet it's either Dolly or Kate. One of them must have seen me come home, and she's nosey about what I bought. Oh, well, if she's sober, she can help me pack.' Dusk had now fallen, and the stoop was in shadows, so she could only distinguish the outline of a male figure at the door. It didn't look like anyone she knew. She straightened her housecoat and smoothed her hair before stepping into the lighted doorway. "Yes?"

"Oh, good evening. I'm Howie Johnson. I've seen you down at the Tavern" and, Cris surreptitiously checked the lock on the screen door. (The harmless little guy, huh?) "I, ah, I thought you two should meet."

Cris took a step closer to the door where she had a better view of the stoop and looked into the face of a tall, muscular, gray-haired man. 'That's him! That's my Dad! Good Lord, now what do I do or say? What if he doesn't recognize me? Maybe he will think, with that other man bringing him here, that I'm an Oh my Lord, what do I do?' These thoughts were chasing themselves round and round in her head. Cris was really flustered. If Howie Johnson introduced them further, she couldn't remember. She hoped they wouldn't notice how shaken she was. Cris had to do something besides standing there gazing at them with her mouth hanging open; she closed her mouth.

The tall man was smiling as he held out a hand toward her containing a picture. 'Why, it's my baby picture! I've got one just like it on the dresser!", it all came out in a breathless rush.'

"Cris," he said gently, "I've been looking for you for a long time." She silently opened the door and stepped aside so they could enter. She forgot the chaotic state of the room, the open half-packed suitcase, the packages, and the general disorder. All she was conscious of was the fact that, at last, she found him. The fact that it was the other way around was inconsequential and unimportant. What was important was that, at last, they were together. She eventually gathered her wits and asked them to sit. Mr. Johnson declined with the excuse, "You two don't need or want me around. I know you have a lot to talk about, so I'll be going along. See you later, Chris." Cris was astonished to hear him speak so familiarly to her, and then she realized he wasn't talking to her; he was talking to her father. "Cris, we have a lot of catching up to do, eh?" She nodded silently in complete agreement. "Cat got your tongue?" he teased. That broke the tension. Cris laughed and then asked shyly, "Would you like coffee? I just made some."

She fled to the kitchen without waiting for an answer and felt she needed something. Coffee would have to do. She didn't have any liquor in the house, and that's what she wanted now. She was shaking like a leaf. 'Get ahold of yourself, old girl. This is what you've been waiting for. Your long search is over.' Thus, mentally scolding herself.

She made her clattering way back to the living room and handed him a half cup and a saucer full of coffee. For a time, they sat in silence and sipped coffee. She watched him pat his jacket pocket in search of something. He drew out his pipe, tapped the tobacco down, and was about to light it when he thought to raise inquiring eyes to his daughter. "Oh, please do." She gave him an ashtray. He puffed contentedly, filling the room with a fragrant odor, then, "Sorry, Cris, I didn't think," as he offered her a cigarette. She shook her head. "Don't smoke, eh?" "I tried it once and almost choked myself." The ice was broken.

They talked until almost daybreak, and it was wonderful. It was all that Cris imagined it to be. She held on to each word he uttered as if it were some rare pearls and watched his every movement with adoring eyes. She watched as though it wasn't real that he was here, and if she didn't watch closely, he would disappear. At times she would reach out to touch him as if to assure herself it was all real. That it was all happening, that they were really together. "You know, I couldn't believe Howie when he said he thought you were little Cris. He said he saw you at the tavern."

"How did he know about me? He just saw me a couple of times." Cris replied.

"Oh, Howie and I have been friends for almost as long as you are old. Anyway, it really wasn't hard to put two and two together for anyone who knew either of us very well. Look." He arose, reaching for her hand to gently pull her to stand beside him, facing the mirror. It was indisputable. Oh, yes, anyone seeing the two faces mirrored together would know.

She thought, 'He's just like I always pictured. A bit older, perhaps, but I can't say I'm too surprised. Leah always had a penchant for older men.' He was tall, almost a foot taller than her, and carried his 220 pounds evenly distributed on a muscular 6'3" frame. Now she knew why she was so tall. Yes, anyone knowing either of them well would know.

Cris was glad they were alone because she could feel the tears stinging her eyes. She didn't want to cry. Now was the time to be happy. Where were all the speeches she had so carefully formulated? She had been so sure that she would be able to handle the occasion with grace and aplomb if and when she met him. Now, here she was blubbering on his big strong shoulder while he alternately patted her back and smoothed her hair. He let her have her cry before pressing his handkerchief into her hand. She noticed his eyes weren't exactly dry either. She cried herself out, and now they could settle down to talk.

They discussed things frankly, even the shamefulness, the unpleasantness, and the shortcomings of each other. It was peculiar, almost uncanny, the way they seemed to know when the other was attempting to evade an issue, and they would ask leading questions of each other to bring out all the details. It seemed they were unable to spare themselves anything.

For instance, how had Chris and Sooky met? Why didn't they marry? Who did the breaking up? Where did Mom fit into the picture? In a word, what is the whole story? As Big Chris talked, Cris called on her storehouse of facts, meager as they were in this department, and was now able to piece together many of the things she already vaguely knew but had, here-to-fore, been unable to fit into the puzzle.ee

Chapter 15

Big Chris began to unfold the story. At times, Cris leaned forward, hands clasped and arms tightly encircling her knees, eyes wide and wondering, body upright and tense, hands clenched into tight balls, eyes hard and flashing. Then she would lean back in her chair with her hands resting quietly in her lap, eyes half-closed, soft, and dreamy. She was a study of emotions.

Sometimes she would be listening calmly and contemplatively only to suddenly change and interrupt impatiently or question angrily. Big Chris would stop, at these times, and wait until her outburst was spent and then explain or answer whatever prompted her to speak. He was truthful and thorough. He found he could hold nothing back in his story and urged Cris to try to understand and forgive in some instances. There were times during his narration when Cris alternated between deep hatred and overwhelming love for the man pacing the floor.

Big Chris told his story:

He met Mamie (that would be Mom) in Idaho. They were both working on a ranch, he was a farmhand, and she was the cook. They had struck up a friendship through their mutual work and interests. Both of them found that they would like to have a place of their own someday. A farm or a chicken ranch but, it would belong to them. Through talking together in the evenings, a conclusion was reached that if they were to pool resources and know-how, they could possibly buy, or at any rate, lease a place. They realized it would be nothing big at first, but they could make it pay off and expand with work. They also knew full well it would mean a lot of hard, back-breaking work, but it would be better than working for someone else.

Chris and Mamie spent long evenings and Sundays scouring the countryside, searching for a small place they could afford. Most of the places were large spreads, much too large for what they had in mind and too expensive for the money they had on hand. They were becoming discouraged, war clouds were on the horizon, and prices were becoming exuberant. It was ironic, but the war was what turned the tide in their favor. Quite a few of the younger people were leaving the farms for the city or entering the army; some of the larger farms were forced to parcel or lease off sections of the land by lack of sufficient farmhands. That was what they were waiting on. They were able to lease a corner of a big spread, complete with a tiny house which they quickly converted into Mamie's much dreamed of chicken house. Some of the ground was already cleared and ready for planting, and there was more, lots more that could be. They were elated, but it would be a hard uphill grind; at least they would be working for themselves.

It wasn't too long before they could see that it would be a success. Even now, they were making a fairly good go of it. He and Mamie worked well together and came to an understanding, nothing definite, exactly, but an understanding, nevertheless.

Now that things were going so well, Mamie wanted to send for her daughter and grandchild (Sooky and Jeanie), which they did. Mamie was proud of her progeny and was ever so anxious to provide distractions for her. Leah just ended a brief marriage, which was one of the reasons for Mamie wanting her near. Leah was an only child, and Mamie worshipped her.

When Mamie was too busy or tired to take Leah around and amuse her, the task fell to Chris. It was flattering and ego-building to squire a pretty dependent young woman around. Mamie was pleased that Chris and Leah hit it off so well. Leah was shy and, like a kid turned loose in a candy store. The hay-rides, sleigh rides, square dances, and even the country's terrain were so different from what she'd known. This life was all new to her.

    She loved to dance, and so did Chris. They would often attend the local dances while Mamie was more than content to stay at home with little Jeanie. If it was a square dance, wild horses couldn't have dragged her away from there. After one such dance, the crowd decided to go on to the neighboring town to "as they said, polish off the night." Leah looked at Chris imploringly. This was all so new and so much fun to her. He knew they should return home, but he agreed to go since the next day was Sunday with not much work to be done. He was treading on thin ice. He knew that he was becoming too aware of Leah as a young-desirable woman and Mamie's daughter. Chris was equally sure he could handle things, at least until Leah had time to become interested in some young buck. He should have sense enough to know that he and Leah, in some ways we're very much alike. Either of them could not pass up the prospect of a challenging conquest. He was sure both of them realized it was just an amusing and harmless game. A game that would be over as soon as Leah found a suitable young man. He didn't know that Leah could put on a good front but was really quite naive and unknowledgeable, in many ways. Leah was infatuated with him. He should have known they were playing with fire. What started in fun, boomeranged. Things got completely out of hand. Leah was pregnant, and he was responsible. Poor trusting Mamie. She was crushed and drained of any emotion, save a deeply loyal, protective devotion to Leah. She knew Leah needed to be protected at any cost, even it meant walking away from a now lucrative business.

They dropped entirely out of sight. The first time he heard from them after they left was when the baby picture arrived. It bore an out-of-state postmark, and as soon as he could make arrangements, he went to the city from which it was mailed. He could find no trace of them, so he returned to the ranch and waited. Maybe one or the other of them would soften and let him know their whereabouts. They didn't. Through a mutual friend, he was able to send a letter. He waited impatiently for an answer. He got it. An unopened letter. That was the way things were. He didn't know what to do or how he could make amends.

As badly as he felt, he knew it must have been tough on both Mamie and Leah. How they both must have suffered. Mamie watching Leah's body swelling day by day and knowing Leah betrayed her trust. Leah, knowing how much she hurt Mamie, not only emotionally, but financially as well. After all, there had been an understanding between Chris and Mamie, and Leah knew it. How did Leah feel? What could she say? Could she possibly explain to Mamie, or would she admit he, Chris was not alone to be blamed? (That was the question neither Big Chris nor Cris would ever get the answer to. The only person who could give it was Mamie, who refused to talk about it ever!!)

He went on to say that he tried all the ways he could think of to find them but to no avail. Occasionally a picture would come, but never a word. Just a picture. He finally gave up and married.

Yes, there were children in his family now. A boy and a girl. No, they were not his own. Dave was a step-son, Mitzie was adopted. Only Dave was home now, and Mitzie was on tour with a dancing troop in California. They were older than Cris, and his

Precocious Brown Eyes

wife knew about her and his long search to find her. She would be so happy to know they finally found each other. He ended with, "I know she'll love you, and I hope you will come to love her too." "I'll just bet we will," Cris thought grimly. She was already highly jealous of him and didn't want to share him with anyone.

Now it was time for Cris to relate her events leading up to this time. She was truthful, holding back nothing. She saw him wince at some parts of her story, and saw the pain in his eyes, and was glad. Glad, not because she was hurting him, but because by making him feel her deprivations and hardships, she was released from some of the bitterness and sense of injustice she lived with. She poured it all out, speaking calmly, hysterically, matter-of-factly, or amusingly. He watched her eyes as she talked emotionally.

He saw the carefree days of early childhood in her eyes, eyes young, gay, and dancing with mischief. She made him see the little brown cracker-box house in the middle of nowhere. He lived and laughed through the shenanigans she lived and racked with delight at her description of joining the Church and being baptized. Chris felt her hurt and knew the frustration she felt about finding him. He was present at her confrontation of Sooky (Leah) and Mom (Mamie) through her eyes, demanding to know all about him. Now her eyes were sharp and piercing. He saw her eyes old and lifeless as she spoke about Sooky's death. Through her eyes, he was a somber witness.

Her eyes went hard, cold as she spoke of her fruitless determination to find him and the futile move she and Mom made to this city years ago.

Her eyes were warily shrewd as if appraising his reaction when telling about her brief marriage and the disastrous dip into the seedy side of life. He experienced her humiliation and desperation of finding herself in jail. Her utter despair on hearing the massive doors clang shut behind her moved him deeply. He agreed with her completely when she fervently said, "Thank God, I got caught so soon I didn't have a chance to become hardened enough to accept being locked in jail. That one time was enough for me." Her eyes were tender and filled with love as she spoke of Mom and the children. Between the tears, some happy, some of the grief and shame, it was all out. It was when they spoke of the future that her eyes became disarmingly naive and child-like.

"Speaking of the future, I think we should both call home and let the families know. I think they should be in on the good news, too, Cris." She called Mom, and he called home. Everyone was excited, elated, and thankful the long search was over.

"Mother' wanted her to come home with her Dad immediately, but Cris begged off, promising to come the next night for dinner and to meet her. The two of them talked almost all night. The day was breaking, and never had Cris seen a more beautiful daybreak. Big Chris left for home, and Cris lay down to get a little sleep before going to work. She found she was much too keyed up to sleep or even relax. She lay there with her eyes closed, thinking and sifting facts, wondering just what their families were thinking and how it would be explained to friends and neighbors. Just how the explanations were made, she would never know.

Although she had gotten little or no sleep that night, her working day flew by like a breeze. She could scarcely wait for the closing bell and practically ran home. Tonight, she was going home with her father for dinner!

She bathed and dressed with the utmost care, discarding many choices before deciding on a simple pink dress, white shoes, gloves, and bag. She should wear a hat, she thought, but that was something she seldom, if ever, wore. She would buy or borrow one. No, it would make her more self-conscious, and tonight would be an ordeal enough without the added complication of wearing a hat. No, no hat. So, she promptly dashed uptown and bought a large white floppy straw hat which made her look quite child-like and innocent.

She was practically sprinting as she left the Hat Shoppe and couldn't afford to be late tonight. She spied a cab and skidded to a stop beside it. Barely waiting for the driver to confirm it was empty, she piled in and slammed the door. She gave her address, glanced anxiously at her watch before leaning back contentedly. Cris would make it on time. Suddenly she jerked upright! A thought flashed in her mind. She must have a gift of some kind. Frantically she signaled the driver to stop and wait for her as she darted pell-mell into a Florist shop. The clerk must have thought her a ninny as she literally grabbed a bouquet of mixed flowers from a display vase and tossed a bill on the counter. She hoped it was enough to cover the cost, but she didn't have the time to barter and wait as a normal shopper did. Cris wasn't about to be late tonight! Tonight, was the night she had been looking forward to for so long to do anything to spoil it.

Despite her impromptu shopping trip, she was ready long before her Dad came to pick her up. Nervously she paced the floor, periodically checking her watch, her appearance in the mirror, and looking out the window. She was glad Mitzie was away. That would make one less opponent, no, that was being unfair to them, but, nevertheless, one less person she would have to meet tonight.

The house was all she could have dreamed or imagined it to be. Large and homey, set in a roomy yard with trees and flowers surrounding it. There was a grape-covered walk in the back and a small fish pond on the side. It was beautiful. It was home. She got out of the car and stood on the sidewalk admiring it.

It was not until she heard a soft voice saying, "Welcome home, Cris," did she notice the plump round smiling woman on the porch. Cris was glued in place; why this woman and Mom could pass for sisters! She became aware of a slight pressure on her arm urging her forward. All of her pre-dislike of her father's wife vanished as she was enfolded in a hearty warm embrace.

They entered the house with arms entwined. It was like coming home, and she didn't feel at all like a stranger. It was just like coming home!

They paused in the hall where Cris shyly presented her flowers. She was glad to have chosen flowers over candy now. Somehow flowers suited the occasion better. Cris feasted her eyes on the wide staircase and the comfortable hospitable living room with its big fireplace. Even the savory smells permeating the house created a picture for her. She closed her eyes and clasped her hands in a gesture very close to supplication. A welcome home indeed! "Dave, how long are you going to primp? You're getting worse than your sisters". The easy way her stepmother accepted her astonished Cris as well as gave her a feeling of peace. "On my way." So that was Dave. Instinctively, she felt drawn to him. She knew they were going to be friends, good friends. He came bounding down the steps to engulf her in a bear hug and planted a kiss on her forehead before holding her at arm's length for inspection. "So, you're little Cris. Mother, she's more like Dad than Dad himself."

Amid the laughter and jokes, the table was cleared, and the dishes washed. Everyone pitched in, although Mother laughingly said she could do it twice as fast without male participation. The meal was delicious. Mother not only looked like Mom but was about as good a cook to boot. She smiled inwardly, thinking Big Chris must not have forgotten Mom entirely.

Next, on the agenda was a tour of the house; Cris was captivated. The house was more than a house. It was a home. She felt more than a twinge of jealousy. It wasn't fair! All these years when she had been struggling, here Mitzi and Dave were enjoying all the comforts of life. Now they had come to a closed-door where Mother reached around her to open it. The door swung open easily on its hinges. The room was breathtakingly lovely—a typical girl's room: crisp ruffled curtains, canopied bed, and chintz-covered rocker. The floor was covered with a colorful flat braided colonial rug. There was even a desk in the corner between the windows with the lamp glowing—a charming girl's room. Cris walked around it slowly, often letting a caressing hand linger on something, but something was missing. The rest of the family stood watching from the doorway. Big Chris broke the silence to ask, "Like it Cris?" "Oh, yes, Mitzi was a very lucky girl and must have been very happy here."

"This isn't Mitzi's room, Cris. We thought you might like it." Now she knew what was missing. It didn't have the air of being lived in. It was all too new. "Cris, this is your room. We want you home, if you'll come," said Mother.

Cris was overcome and wanted desperately to cry but was determined not to spoil the evening by weeping, so she walked out the door saying as gaily as she could, "now let's see the rest of the house." The tour over, they returned to the living room for coffee and more talk before Cris left for home. During this time, Cris studied a picture of Mitzie furtively.

It wasn't until they returned to the living room that Cris looked at the pictures on the mantle. There are some of me! "Does that answer your question of how Howie knew you?" her Dad asked. She nodded and smiled self-consciously. There was her baby picture, one of her with her pet cat. She was all legs. Oh no, not one of her baptizing. She laughed aloud, remembering. The last was of her in the uniform of her school orchestra. She looked at the pictures with a puzzled expression. Big Chris told her he didn't know where they were all those years, and yet here were pictures to refute his story. As if he could read her thoughts, Big Chris took the pictures and removed them from the frames before handing them to her while saying, "Turn them over and see when I got them and where they came from." On the back of each of them was a date, and only one was from any place Chris had ever been, Wyoming. The one of her and her cat was from Chicago. Mr. Benson must have mailed it when he attended that convention. The one from Texas obviously had been sent through the care of Mom's relatives. The Alaska one stymied her for a while. Then came the dawn! Kurt could have mailed it when he visited Sooky when she was ill before leaving on a fishing trip. "As I said, I tried, but there was no way I could go to all the places and search."

He left the room and returned with a packet of worn envelopes. Some contained the original photos, and some were answers to queries Big Chris made in search of them. Cris studied the rest of the family pictures, especially Mitzi. Gee, she was pretty and so graceful. This must have been a recent photo. She was in costume and was posed elegantly against a background of tall white pillars. The massiveness of the pillars served to accentuate her small curvaceous figure. She was beautiful. Looking at her, Cris felt dowdy, misshapen, enormous, and gawky. Mitzie was so graceful, poised, and talented. They must be very proud of her. She remembered how she pictured herself growing up to be petite and lovely, like Mitzi as a small child. If her inner thoughts or envy of Mitzi were apparent, no one appeared to notice.

Chapter 16

The newness of having a family complete with a Dad was extremely exciting to Cris. Now, though she still called Mom and the children very frequently, her visits to them became less frequent because she spent more and more time with her newfound family.

One evening, after dinner, Big Chris announced that Mitzi would be coming home for a visit. "Now," he said, "all the family will be together." He paused and looked at Cris, "together and at home if you would move home. There's plenty room, and we'd all love to have you, you know." This request had been made a number of times before, and Cris always hesitated, but with Mitzi coming home, maybe she would. After all, why should she continue to let Mitzi have most of her dad's time and attention? Cris was positive that she was coming home because Big Chris told her about finding Cris.

Cris wanted to have the rest of their lives to share. The way she figured it, Mitzi already had more than her share. She was about to say yes to the move, it would be nice, but she reconsidered. Maybe she and Mitzi should meet first. Maybe Mitzi would not accept her as readily as Dave and 'Mother' had. She was sure she wouldn't accept Mitzi. Anyway, she would only be home for a short time. It might be well to feel things out first.

Cris was nervous, uptight, and consumed with jealousy. If she could have gracefully or tactfully arranged it, she would not have promised to be present for the homecoming dinner for Mitzi. She was determined to be as poised and gracious as Mitzi's picture made her appear to be. No, Cris was not going to be the one to show her claws first, but if she sensed any animosity from Mitzi, she was sure to hold her own.

Finally, the big day arrived. Cris was a nervous wreck. At work, she made mistake after mistake. Finally, she asked for time off. Her boss, knowing something was wrong, assumed she received bad news about the children. When Cris wouldn't elaborate, she was let off with much sympathy and told to be sure to call if there was anything they could do or if she needed more time off.

Cris must have changed clothes a dozen times before picking out just the right outfit. After what seemed hours, it was time to catch her cab and go home. ("How long can I call it home?" she thought.)

Before Cris could get out of the cab, Mitzi was there, giving her one of the biggest smiles and a great big bear hug! "Hi Sis. You don't know how long I have been waiting to say those words!" Mitzi completely disarmed Cris. She seemed genuinely happy to see her! And Cris wasn't prepared for this. She didn't know whether to accept Mitzi or be wary of what she was up to. Sensing Cris' discomfort, Mitzi put her arm around Cris and continued to talk into the house. The rest of the family was waiting at the door with big smiles of approval. Mitzi asked Cris many questions, and they tumbled out without giving Cris a chance to answer many of them. The whole family was chatting like this was just an ordinary family dinner by the time dinner ended. Cris felt a comfortable feeling she never had before. She wasn't used to being a part of such a loving, caring family.

She and Mitzi got to be great pals. She missed Jeannie more than she thought, and Mitzi not only filled that longing, but being a little closer to her age had more in common with her. Needless to say, Mitzi was the one to convince Chris to move "home."

Cris was sorry when it was time for Mitzi to go back on the road. She wondered what she was going to do without her pal. However, before the time was up for Mitzi to leave, she begun to talk to Cris about joining her troop as an extra and part-time costume arranger. Cris loved to dance, and Mitzi could show her some of the simpler routines they performed. Cris was also very good at sewing, designing, blending colors and could be a real asset. The pay was more than Cris ever made, and the life seemed to be exciting. It was another change that just might prove to be a challenge and help Cris find her niche in life.

Before agreeing to go with Mitzi, Cris made a trip home to see about Mom and the children. Had she not been so engrossed in her new family and new life; she might have noticed that there was an undercurrent of trouble brewing at home. Oh, on the surface, things seemed to be going well. She explained to Mom how this would be an exciting life for her. She would also be able to send more money along with the child support they received from 'Sonny boy,' the children should be much better off. Maybe they could even move into a larger place where each of the girls could have their own room. Ella was getting ready to begin school, and Ann could now sleep in a room by herself with her many stuffed animals and dolls.

Mom looked at her sadly. She didn't say anything to the contrary. She may have felt some guilt for keeping Cris from her father all these years. Maybe she also felt sorry for the poverty they had been in when Cris could have had a more affluent life with her other family. Perhaps, she'd never seen Cris so radiant and did not want to add any pain or sorrow. Whatever the reason, she agreed with Cris that this was an opportunity she should not miss.

On the road with Mitzi, Cris found it was not all fun and games. She had to WORK! She sent money and cards to Mom and the girls very frequently at first, but as her duties increased, she began to have less and less contact with them. She didn't even appear to notice that Mom wasn't writing as frequently, and sometimes the letters seemed to be in someone else's handwriting. What was happening back home was that Mom was going blind! The girls were small, and she was doing the best she could to continue taking care of them. The neighbors began to notice the girl's clothing was not kept as clean as it had been in the past. Mom was always an excellent housekeeper, but now there was always clutter and dust. Poor Mom, she still refused to contact Cris to let her know what was happening. Jeannie had a son a couple of years older than Ella. He would come by and do chores for her and report back to his mom from time to time. Jeannie tried to get Mom and the girls to stay with her, but Mom insisted she could do for herself and them and didn't want to strain Jeannie's marriage. She also refused to give Jeannie Cris's address or any way to reach her. Finally, someone reported the family's situation to the Health Department, and they sent a social worker out to investigate. Mom was adamant that she could care for herself and the girls and needed no interference; thank you! However, without any of Mom's assistance, they were able to contact 'Sonny Boy,' who was living in another state and remarried. He contacted Mom and, without telling her anything, asked to speak to Cris. When Mom simply told him she wasn't in, he asked for a time when he could talk to her. Poor Mom didn't know what to say. After a few daily phone calls from him, Mom finally told him that Cris was temporarily out of town on business.

'Sonny Boy' had been sending support for the children regularly, even though Cris only sometimes wrote back or sent pictures. Now, he wrongly assumed that Cris was taking that money and traveling, or partying or whatever, and his children were being taken care of by a blind old lady who needed care herself. He was livid and contacted the authorities and told them he hadn't known of the conditions his children were living in. He informed them he would be on the next train to pick them up. 'Sonny Boy' asked that they not tell Mom until he arrived, thinking she might hide them. (He was right in his thinking!) The State would have to make them wards of the court and they had no desire to add on two more children if there was an alternative, so they agreed.

By the time Mom could notify Cris, the children were gone, Jeannie moved Mom in with her, and Mom was totally blind. Cris was devastated and didn't know what to do. She blamed herself, her new family, Mom, and everyone and everything she could. She, of course, came home immediately, but there was nothing she could do. The State told her they could do nothing about the children because they were now in another state. They said unless there were a complaint about their care, they would remain with their father and stepmother.

Mom (or Gram as the children renamed her) had surgery on her eyes but could never see again. Cris never went on the road again. She spent the rest of Mom's life caring for her. Oh, yes, she heard from the girls from time to time but was not allowed to have any unsupervised visits with them. Cris kept in contact with her Dad until he finally passed away from cancer. She did not spend much time with him or the family because Mom (Gram) felt uncomfortable being around them because of their previous relationship. "May's well let dead dogs lie," Mom said. "He got a new family and makin' a good life for them, don' need me messing him up with memories that don' mean nothing no more." Eventually, she drifted out of touch with Mitzi, Dave, and Mother. 'Gram' became her whole life. She was her eyes, and she tried to fill the gap left by the girls and the heartache. Gram never got over the passing of Sooky.

Over the years, Cris had taken classes in business and nursing. She worked as a paralegal, a nurse's assistant, and became a good nurse. The girls had grown up and were married with families of their own. Now, retired, she lived alone with Baron. "You know," she thought, 'it has really been a full and challenging life. You know, Baron, I think I'll write a book about my life. It just might be interesting to my grandchildren. Times have changed so much, and I want them to know how it was back then and how we got from there to here.'

And so began another change in the life of Cris.

About the Authors

Marian Christine Hunt was born in Casper, Wyoming, on March 18, 1919. She was raised in Seattle and Tacoma, Washington. Marian did minimal traveling but was a voracious reader; she learned about many parts of the country and world. Ms. Hunt decided to write this book several years before passing away in 1996. While this book is fiction, many of the incidents and places mentioned came from her early recollections of what life was like growing up in this area.

Gloria McSwain King is the eldest daughter of Marian and co-author of this book. After Marian's death, her daughter correlated the papers Marian had so meticulously labored over. Like her mother, she is a voracious reader, and her five children all love reading. Gloria is the biological mother of three sons, two daughters, one adopted son, several foster and has raised several of her relative's children. She is currently retired and resides in Seattle, Washington.

Made in the USA
Las Vegas, NV
01 November 2021